Like a Queen

by Constance Hall

Like a Queen Pty Ltd

I would like to thank first and foremost beautiful Bill, for putting up with me and allowing me to share the most intimate parts of our life, Bill worked his arse off to help me get this book out, I couldn't ask for a more supportive man.

My darling children, they have sacrificed mum time in a life that already saw me spread thinly, they filled in the gaps and helped each other when mum was too busy.

My sister Stella for being my biggest fan and reading everything I have ever written since I was a little kid, well before my blogs, well before anyone else cared, she always did.

My brothers, for pretty much nothing, but I love the selfish arseholes.

To my mum for being the woman that I needed her to be, for teaching me social justice and for being proud of who we are.

Thank you to my step dad, my humble old step dad for trusting me and helping me wherever he could.

My uncles and aunties for your endless support, you guys are everything. Family is everything and I am a women rich in family.

My girl crush and agent Nerida Moore, whose skills have gone far above and beyond what a normal manager should do, from marriage counselling to life coaching, Ned is my rock, my mentor, in a world where I have felt people trying to change me constantly, she has always encouraged me to above anything else, trust my instincts and just be me. I thank my lucky stars she came into my life.

My beloved dad. Not a day goes by that I don't imagine the pride that would appear on your face if I had the chance to hand you a book that I wrote. I bet you can see me now and I bet you're proud as fuck. Thank you for being you, the most loving man I have ever met, thank you for flooding your daughters' lives with love and self worth. I love you.

ISBN 978-0-646-95949-8
Publishing Facilitator: Kristen Watts
Sub Editor: Stephanie Pegler
Photography: Ben Proposch Shooting Light Photography
Design: Rachel Pepper – www.rachelpepper.com
Hair and Makeup: Elicia Rudd
Cover image shot on location in Western Australia
Note: some names have been changed to protect privacy

This book is dedicated to my Queens, you made this happen.
I am eternally grateful.

What you see in others is what you see in yourself.

Yep, another old cliche, thanks Con. But this little gem is a truthful one and will be your only real tool in recognising that you have reached Queendom.

Queens see Queens. They don't see weight problems, they don't see crazy bitches, they don't see failures.

I thought there was something in the water, like women everywhere had changed, when I first started seeing divinity everywhere I went — a mum getting out of her car ... radiating, the girl making my coffee ... glowing, the woman pushing a supermarket trolley with a huge fuck-my-life expression ... goddess. Queens everywhere.

One day I was drinking a soy chai and watching two women chatting and enjoying a coffee while simultaneously rocking babies and wrestling toddlers. They looked so beautiful, so wise, so strong, that I nearly cried. I thought I must be pregnant but I wasn't.

It wasn't the women who had changed, it was me.

Then I started talking to women about other women we knew, but not the typical bitchy gossipy crap. I would talk about how beautiful they were, how strong they were and before I knew it, other women came to me to talk about women we knew in the same light, full of love, full of compassion, brainstorming ways that we could help new mums and laughing at the awesomeness of experienced ones.

Love and Compassion breeds Love and Compassion at phenomenal rates.

This is your confirmation that you are truly a Queen, you are what you see in others.

Queens only see Queens. You are a Queen.

CHAPTER 1
The Queen is Crowning

Tock tick, tock tick, tock tick. What's that sound? Oh, that's the sound of time going backwards, because that is quite frankly the only thing time is capable of doing at the end of a pregnancy.

You've reached that point where every single fuck you've accumulated over the three trimesters has now been gracefully drop-kicked out the window.

It's nearly over babe, you're doing so well.

You don't care about what you're eating after trying to be good all pregnancy. Now you're stealing food off everyone and stuffing it in your mouth as fast as you can. Only you kind of feel like you've had gastric lap-band surgery because you can't nearly fit as much food in your tummy as your inner-fat cow desires.

You're gaining three kilos a day, have resorted to wearing a muumuu and towels don't go all the way around you.

If you're anything like me, you also have what I refer to as "hormone nose", where your nose gains its own eight kilograms and takes over your face — it could be fluid, it could be stolen cake.

You can't stand your partner — the sound of him breathing makes you want to smother his face with a pillow. He forgets to ask if you're OK, you download divorce papers (yes, I know they can be downloaded because yes, I downloaded them). He asks if you're OK, you're packing your bags.

Then you read a story online about some poor lady whose husband died and you run to your man crying, kissing him and begging him not to die.

So basically you're just a really big, hungry mental patient.

All the ads and TV shows, even your friends' Facebook accounts, seem to depict this strange handsome boyfriend creature who rubs pregnant bellies waiting for the baby to kick, excited for the baby's arrival.

Being part of that loving smug relationship has been a dream of yours since you were a teenager. Yet now that you're here, your reality is this Big Foot doppelganger who's already had a six-pack of beer. The smell of his beer breath is bringing back your morning sickness and his snoring is DRIVING YOU NUTS.

There is no love, just a sweaty pregnant chick and a man she wants to punch.

Marital Bliss.

If you have other kids, your patience for them is lost, too. In my last trimester with my twins Rumi and Snow, I couldn't even get up off the couch. When I heard an injustice between my two other kids, I would simply scream. Like a dying whale in a sea of her own filth, lying on the couch screaming "Arlo!!!! Give her back her tiger teddy!" and seconds later "Billie-Violet!! If you just kicked your brother, I'm calling your dad and when he gets home from work there will be huge consequences!!"

Obviously my kids really gave a shit as they continued to torment each other while I cried on the couch. I actually lost my voice most weeks. Screaming at kids, screaming at the dog, screaming at the remote control I couldn't reach. So glamorous.

And just to leave you and your family in a constant state of emotional confusion, the hormonal wave of ecstasy-love crashes over you and you haul that huge arse off your couch-nest, and head into their rooms where you freak the shit out of them with love, compliments, head sniffing and massages until they fall asleep. Once your parental guilt kicks in — the comedown — you loathe yourself for your usual lack of patience, while you watch them sleep, love them to bits, hate yourself until you fall asleep and wake up in time to hate your kids again. Fun!!!!

So it's needless to say that well before my due date even rolled around, I was holding a group meeting trying to elect which lucky friend was short-strawing the exclusive rights to come over, glove up and break my waters. COME ON LABOUR.

No Takers... selfish molls.

A Queen can give birth any which way she wants.

It's pretty simple, unless you want to push a baby the size of a dragon egg out of your vagina for me, you don't get to judge, comment or advise. Unless you want to tell me what an incredible rock-star-birther fertility-Queen you believe I am, your opinion is void.

Queens need an empire of understanding and support when ruling the unknown. Some crave privacy, turn inside themselves and draw strength from solitary wisdom while others need support from every angle. Like my psychologist, Jasmine, said to me: "You, Constance, need a team of support."

Her words became gospel to me from that day on. Team Constance consisted of a GP, a psych, my mother, all of my friends (real ones and Facebook ones), my partner Bill, his friends and any poor bitch I walked past on the street. Go Team!

The Empire of a Queen must be full, enriched and in a constant state of growing.

There are so many categories, styles and avenues to take when birthing. I am mainly drawing from personal experiences when I squash the Western way into three different plans. (I say plans because we all know that you can plan to birth any which way you like — the reality is that a hell of a lot of birth plans don't go to plan.)

1. Earth Mother

An Earth Mother is a total goddess — she wants to feel it, wants to experience the divine journey. Earth Mothers can give birth in a tree, being drip-fed essential oils from a kookaburra's beak, or in a hospital bed with her obstetrician/ spirit animal. She can produce a five-kilogram Dalai Lama reincarnate and still require no intervention.

Earth Mother comes in many different forms — the only common thread is these women do not need drugs.

It can be a home birth with a doula or just her boyfriend, or some Earth Mothers are complete divas and want a massive audience of spirit minions to watch and fulfill her demands. And so she should: what Earth Mother wants, Earth Mother gets, because Earth Mother is a warrior.

There are so many different individual dynamics to an Earth Mother. Basically if you don't want drugs or intervention, to me you are Earth Mother and you are worthy of every bit of praise that comes your way.

Chuck in some previous kids to take a leisurely swim in the after-birth-filled birthing spa and we have a complete fucking commune of awesome powerhouse Earth-birthing.

There will be spiritual channelling, sage sticks, a husband in the laundry pulling a bucket bong, and bang, we have a baby.

I am being extreme, the average Earthy is actually just a really hot sexy bitch with a spa and an ambition. She believes in herself; she believes in her body, its power and its god-given right to carry out the job it is designed to do. Hats are off and Queenies are bowing down to Earthy Birther, legendary status.

The Earth Mother cannot be fucked with another human telling her humanly body how to push a human out of her vajoots, she is drawing on the strength of our ancestors. Just because I need a Valium to even talk about giving birth does not mean for one second that I'm not completely riddled with extreme jealousy over Earthy's strength and bravery. I kiss the ground she walks on, I just think she's crazy for doing so and would appreciate that she doesn't judge the drug coma I like to be in while birthing.

There are many reasons why I would never entertain the idea of Earth-birthing. The main one would have to be due to my unintentional brush with labour pains during my first birth.

I was twenty-five years old, I had been with Bill for almost a year when I fell pregnant and I had absolutely no idea what I was doing. Like many young women, I was totally unaware of my royal status, I felt about as queenly as a dead cockroach and it showed. Pregnancy had worn me down, no longer participating in a party-animal binge-drinking lifestyle meant I felt truly lost, as if my identity had disappeared.

Throughout the forty weeks, I was shocked at the lack of fucks given to me regarding my pregnancy. In my mind I was riding an elephant through town with servants holding beaded umbrellas over my head because … Hello I was pregnant. But in reality, if it wasn't for my hourly updates on Facebook, nobody would have noticed. I certainly wasn't getting offered seats on the bus or having strangers handing me ice-creams like I expected.

My entire pregnancy was kind of like one big anti-climax. One minute I was a gorgeous young party animal and the next I felt sick, couldn't drink booze and couldn't find my crown.

It had been a few years since I had even gone to see a doctor for yet another case of chlamydia, which felt unavoidable in my youth. I know what you are all thinking, has the dirty bitch ever heard of a condom? Well, the answer was yes but when you were a people-pleasing desperado who was overjoyed that a guy was even prepared to bang her, if he didn't want to use a condom, my unqueenly self wasn't about to complain.

How times have changed. Unfortunately, I am not single now to show off my arse-kicking self-assurance to a brand-new erection but I can live vicariously through my single friends.

One night when I was thirty-five weeks pregnant, in bed no doubt feeling sorry for myself in my sleep, I was woken up at 1am by what I thought was my bladder failing. I went to sit up and another gush of water spilled out of my Pleasure Paddock and on to the sheets. I nudged Bill, who rolled over after uttering the following comment: "Wake me up if anything else happens."

Feeling alone and scared, I called the hospital.

When you're having your first baby, you think the entire world revolves around you. Every time someone calls, you think it's to hear about the miracle growing inside your tummy, you don't status update unless it's about your incredible journey, you send out group messages to keep everyone informed, you have baby showers and politely tell everyone what you need and so on and so on. It's a big fucking deal.

So prepare yourself for the shock of all holy shock-horrors when you realise that nobody gives a flying fuck that you are in labour. That's right Queens, you'll wake your hubs, he'll just roll over. You'll call the hospital, they'll tell you to call back when things get more exciting. You'll feel like that little girl all dressed up in her party dress who got the day wrong, all ready and excited, yet all alone.

This was my fork, my very first fork in the road ... Since becoming a mother every single day has presented me with a fork in the road, a choice to sink or swim. Am I going to be a mother who drowns in her own loneliness? Because once you've embarked on the journey of motherhood, loneliness is waiting for you at every corner, every little failure or hiccup or day of overwhelming tiredness is there nudging you further into the corner of loneliness.

Or will I demand help, tell those fuckers that I am here and I am having a goddamn baby and I will not be ignored.

Wake The Fuck Up People! There is a human trying to get out of my body and we want to be worshipped the way we deserve to be.

At least that's what I would do now …

After calling the hospital to make the announcement that my waters had broken and I had lost my mucus plug, I realised there was no chauffeur-driven ambo waiting patiently to roll out the red carpet. Instead I had a midwife on the other end of the phone telling me to come in after about an hour.

So I packed up my things and printed out my birth plan, so efficient.

I wrapped up my mucus plug in a cloth nappy (which was officially the first and last time I ever used a cloth nappy) and packed it into my hospital bag. Now I am not entirely sure why I did this, to be honest I don't even remember packing it, maybe I was unsure if it was normal and felt the need to run it past a nurse — it did look like an oyster — or maybe I was proud or worried that I'd suffer separation anxiety if I didn't bring it. What I do remember is the look on the midwives' faces after I handed it to them and they unwrapped it.

It very suddenly dawned on me that wrapping up the oyster and bestowing it on the midwives was absolutely unnecessary and left me feeling as though I had just served someone up an old used tampon for breakfast.

By the time I dragged Bill out of bed and got to hospital, I was in actual labour and was shitting myself. Maybe it's the bright lights, maybe it's the crabby old midwives, but the assertive, sassy knocked-up chick I thought I was crumbled in a heap of pain while vulnerability washed over me.

I arrived clutching my birth plan. It was typed not handwritten, this I believed signified one having one's shit together. It was an official-looking typed birth plan, not something I'd quickly scrawled on the back of a bus ticket.

I offered it to the woman who looked like the pack leader of the midwives. She didn't even read it. She simply placed it down on the bench and seemed to scoff at it. Is she serious? Did she care that little for my wishes that she couldn't even humour me and read the fucking plan?

Now I'm sure these midwives were all frantically busy but in my mind, they were scrunching up my birth plan into tiny little spit balls and one by one hurling them at me. I hated them.

Had any of the midwives bothered to actually read my birth plan, they would have seen that the entire thing was limited to one glorious sentence in capital letters: "I WANT DRUGS, AND I WANT THEM WITHOUT JUDGMENTS."

No shit, that is all my birth plan said.

The next twelve hours went something like this: I scream, I beg for drugs, midwife rolls her eyes, midwife administers tiny amount of drugs, I keep screaming and so on and so on.

Bill was no help at all. He actually managed to surprise me with the extent of his uselessness. He kept trying to LEAVE … I know right? I already have abandonment issues and Bill tried to abandon me in my time of fucking need with excuses like "I better go and feed the dog" or "I need to put a load of washing on".

By now even the midwives who had made it pretty clear that they hated me were on Team Con.

I was crying and begging Bill to sort me out some pain relief. I wasn't feeling contractions with breaks to recover, I was experiencing constant excruciating agony. Bill was being too fucking reasonable and listening to the midwives advising him that "it's better if she can just keep going without an epidural, she's come this far". I felt so ignored, I distinctly remember feeling like a paralysed animal whose wishes were being ignored.

At one point a midwife turned to me and said "what did you expect it to feel like? You are giving birth."

Well, I didn't expect to feel anything at all, I clearly covered that in my birth plan. You know, the drugs bit!

It's all fine to look back and laugh, after all laughter is the key to happiness and if I couldn't laugh I would break. However, at the time, there was nothing funny about being in agony, nothing funny about feeling like you had nobody on your side, nobody in your corner demanding drugs on your behalf.

Lying in that hospital bed on that day at twenty-five years old, I was unarmed and it taught me a very valuable lesson on self-defence. I would never feel unarmed again.

If only I knew then what I know now about my sisterhood, I would have taken my army into that birthing suite.

I am not sharing this to freak anyone out. I am sharing this story because I want to point out how badly things can go for a Queen who's lost her way, a Queen who can't see her own power, a Queen who's left her crown at home. Delivering my first daughter was my ultimate low point. Without the lows I'd have nothing to offer others, so we as Queens have to embrace the tough times and remember that we are only offered our lows in this life to facilitate reaching out a hand to other Queens in need, being able to empathise over what they may be going through.

Reminding yourself of this while a baby's head is halfway out of your fanny is next to impossible — hindsight is a glorious thing.

The midwives convinced me that I had no choice but to push through the pain, insisting I reach seven centimetres dilated before I could have an epidural. To someone with my pain threshold, you might as well have skinned me alive.

By the time they finally gave me an epidural, it was too late. I felt no pain relief at all. I felt so betrayed by the whole ordeal and pretty much wanted to curl up and die. I know I am inclined to over-dramatise my situations but I could look you right in the eyes now and tell you that I wholeheartedly wanted to die. The baby wasn't coming and I lost any energy to fight.

Even Bill noticed and asked me why I had given up. I turned away from him, feeling sad, let down and furious. Unsupportive midwives had convinced him that I wasn't good enough for this labour, that I couldn't do it and had given up. Just when I needed motivation to find my courage, I received judgment and betrayal.

The doctors had obviously seen this before and decided to whisk me away for a C-section. They shaved my bush and were about to push me into theatre when they noticed my daughter's heart rate had dropped. Without wasting any time, they sliced the biggest episiotomy that went pretty much all the way down to my bum, yanked around the forceps and pulled out my purple little conehead. And just like that, the worst experience of my life was over.

Billie-Violet was premature and had some breathing difficulties so she was urgently taken away, Bill left to feed the dog, my mum left to pick up my brothers from school. I'm sure cleaning me up or wheeling me into another room was someone's responsibility but for all I knew that someone was snorting the drugs that they didn't give me in the toilets somewhere because I was alone, forgotten about.

I have a distinct memory of lying there, covered in my own blood, completely frail in the birthing suite, my baby gone, body torn and feeling betrayed. Betrayed by the whole fucking system. In my delirious, sleep-deprived state, I even imagined that on her way out the door, a midwife turned to me and blew one last spit ball of my invisible birth plan right between my eyes. What a bitch.

I knew, even in my confused state, that it wasn't supposed to be like that.

2. DUV (Drugged Up Vaginal)
This, might I add, is my personal favourite.

DUV mums are in a bit of a limbo, people always ask if you're going "natural"? DUV mums don't really know how to answer. "Well yes, I am having a natural birth", while thinking to themselves, "yes, there will be a baby passing through my vaginal passage … with more drugs in my system than a Black Sabbath after-party. I guess that's pretty natural."

There is actually a hell of a lot of Earth Mothers in this section, Earthies who planned an earth-birth and halfway through were like "umm, what the actual fuck was I thinking? You have to be on crack to sustain this shit when you have reasonable options. An epidural is a reasonable option, bring me that motherfucking needle." They are NOT failed Earth Mothers, they are enlightened Earth Mothers who have simply changed direction, Queens are in a constant state of change.

Changing one's mind based on new information acquired is an essential part of Queenhood.

DUV mums are intuitive, there are no flies on them. These bitches want the baby out, minimal pain and minimal recovery. They say yes to all the extras. Epidural? Thank you. Induction? Don't mind if I do. Gas? Just a glorified nang, bring it.

My second labour, the one I had with Arlo, was a DUV and it was heaven.

After the world's worst experience of giving birth to Billie-Violet, I knew things had to change. I researched and asked everyone I knew, I wanted to know who enjoyed their labour and why.

I came to a very poignant conclusion — I was fucking right the first time!!! Happiness comes in a little needle being inserted into our backs. For my relationship with birthing, happiness is definitely a drug. BAM!

So I searched far and wide to find the right doctor for me and I found him.

Doctor Heart had huge hands (I don't know why but that seemed important), he was handsome and he was servicing some of the poshest bitches in town. Now that included me.

Now we all know I'm not a posh bitch, however I am an incredibly anxious one so if I have to remortgage my house and pretend to be one to win the services of this glorious big-handed doctor, then so be it.

I made my appointments, told him every detail about my first labour and made sure he understood what a nervous wreck I was at the thought of ever waddling down a labour ward corridor again.

So Doctor Heart devised a plan. To calm my anxiety and help me gain a sense of control, we decided to induce my labour a week before my due date. The best part of this plan was that a full-blown epidural would be inserted into my back before I was even induced.

I still tingle when I repeat to myself his wise healing words: "Constance, if you don't want to feel anything, you don't have to."

I trusted Doctor Heart and I was not let down.

Naturally, it wasn't long before his entire clinic realised I was faking it as a posh bitch. I'd walk into the waiting room surrounded by calm, harmonious pregnant posh bitches and while waiting for my appointment, I'd get on my phone, forget where I was and start yelling at Bill.

"YOU HAVE BEEN DRUNK FOR TWO DAYS NOW. TWO MOTHERFUCKING DAYS!!!"

Stunned silence followed. My non-posh-bitch status had been rumbled. But I didn't give two fucks because I was getting the service I had always wanted.

On my induction day, I smugly cruised into hospital with Bill and draped myself over the bed where some of the best drugs I've ever had awaited me on a silver platter. I was strapped up and injected. Once I was completely off my head and numb, they began to induce me. By this point I was so loved up, they could have told me they were slicing off my legs and feeding the pieces to Doctor Heart and I would have just blown them a kiss.

Blessed is the woman who fist pumps during labour.

I can honestly tell you from the bottom of my heart that I enjoyed every second of giving birth to Arlo. I didn't have to do anything and I love not doing anything — it's seriously my favourite thing to do, so this birth suited me to a tee. No catches, no punchlines, just a blissful, smooth two-hour labour where a handsome doctor appeared at the end, pulled a baby out of my fanny and slapped it on my chest. Heaven.

It was only after Arlo was out that I noticed something very awkward. There was poo all over the floor. I knew it was my poo because I had been on these iron pills for the last few months to boost my iron levels. The iron pills made my poo a very distinct shade of black.

The poo in question, on the labour ward floor and on the bed, was that same shade.

Kind of mortified that a cleaner was wiping it up in front of me while I sat there, still too drugged up to move, I whispered to her: "Did I poo on my sexy doctor?"

She pretended she didn't hear me.

Bill, on the other hand, happily interjects with "yes honey, you shat on your sexy doctor. I guess you're stuck with me." Killjoy.

Here is the thing about birth poo. In fact, I could dedicate a whole book to birth poo because it's such a big fucking deal to women. We can handle everything — we can lose loads of blood, we can have giant needles in our backs, we can be raced off for an emergency C-section, but if someone mentions a birth poo … we are stopped in our tracks.

So this needs to be said, the faeces that pass a Queen's anal passage while she gives life are completely and unarguably holy — a holy turd. Any human who it could possibly touch is blessed. To poo during labour is good luck, it is kind of like rubbing a Buddha's belly. If you happen to be graced by the appearance of birth poo, you need to thank your lucky stars, god or Oprah.

Your new baby, your doctor, your husband, yourself and anyone else lucky to be present during your birth poo is touched, now and forever.

Embrace the poo, push as hard as you can, get that poo out. The birth poo-er is WINNING.

If only someone had shared this pearl of wisdom before I pooed on my hot doctor's tight blue latex gloves, it would have saved me a lot of heartache.

The birth poo is but a symbol of a woman's might, of her strength and determination to do what is best for her baby. A woman who has put aside her dignity and poos on anyone who stands in the way to ensure the safe arrival of her young defines Queenhood.

There is NOTHING as dignified as that.

3. The Planned C-sec

Of all the birthers, this is the least fucks given, flipping the bird at the haters, city birther on a mission. She is a hero and a voice for anyone who has ever asked "umm hang on? It's 2016 ... I don't wanna push a baby out of my Pleasure Paddock. Do I really have to?"

Well that's debatable, some public hospitals in Australia say "yes, you do have to push", while most private hospitals in Australia say "no babe, you can do as you please". On a side note, this gives me the shits, shouldn't we all have the same options and rights when giving birth? #inequalitysucks

If you are going public and want a planned Caesarean, nothing is stopping you from rocking up to the hospital in tears, begging, pleading and insisting that you get your C-section. I have friends who did this, along with some doctor's notes about their severe anxiety, bladder control issues etc. They succeeded. There is no harm in trying.

The planned C-section mum books in her chosen birth date, can pretty much choose her baby's star sign, not that it matters because this type of mum couldn't give two fucks about star signs, she's got a life to live. She wants the baby out pronto so she can introduce it to the wonderful world of long lunches, fulfilling careers and Louis Vuitton nappy bags.

Some Planned Cs can go on to Earth Motherly breastfeed their child for years while some have an injection to ban milk from ever forming anywhere near her breasts because "Fuck Breastfeeding". The Planned C makes her own rules, and then breaks them whenever she sees fit.

The Planned C-sec is the modern-day birthing legend, paving the way for any women who have ever felt judged or ashamed.

I went back to Doctor Heart when I realised I was pregnant again, of course I did. The only thing I was looking forward to about the whole experience was my platter of drugs at the end.

I arrived to see him with a really warm welcome from all the Queens who work in the surgery, obviously all delighted to see me fat and miserable again.

The minute I found out I was having twins, I was offered a Caesarean, apparently you are even more likely to spend the rest of your life Laugh-weeing, Sneeze-weeing and Cough-weeing if you push out twins. So I embraced my inner Too-Posh-to-Push mentality and booked it in.

Obviously, the pregnancy was utter misery, I can't even handle one baby without crying every day so with two babies, my family wanted to build me a cage to live in in the backyard, nice and far away from the rest of the house.

I am not proud to admit that around halfway through this pregnancy, I began begging Doctor Heart to take them out early. From thirty weeks, my uterus became really aggro and started giving me constant contractions trying to get the babies out. I was under doctor's orders to take it as easy as possible to keep them in, which was hard to tell my family and friends, considering I had already lied to them about being under strict bed rest instructions ever since my first trimester just to get out of doing shit.

However, Doctor Heart refused to take them out before thirty-seven weeks unless I went into full-blown labour. Of course looking back, I am grateful and embarrassed that I was so eager to get them out early — not my finest parenting hour.

If it was possible to fail at giving birth, this would be my second fail. But it's not, so this is my second redirection from plan. My body gave up at thirty-four weeks. After calling the hospital every day for months convinced I was going into labour, by this point the ladies on the labour ward were so over me that they were almost as relieved as I was that it was finally happening.

I was the size of a house, both babies were big for their gestation, bigger than your average singleton, and I had spent every day of the last month crying on the couch.

At 4am on October 17, 2014, it was actually happening. I knew this because my waters had erupted and after forty-six false alarms, I knew one thing — the only way the midwives would take me seriously was if my waters had broken.

There was no way I was waiting for my mum to get here and babysit or for Bill to get out of bed and pack up his shit — Bill is a slow man. So I woke him up, standing over him in my nightie with the keys in my hands, a psycho-ward look in my eyes, and told him I was driving myself to hospital. Bill gave me a sympathetic look and said he'd be right behind me.

I sped down the freeway, screaming as my waters flooded the car seat. I was positive I would give birth to the twins on the side of the road and then probably die. I was in agony, fearing that the first twin was crowning and would get stuck underneath my accelerator.

Somehow I made it to the hospital, alive, still with the babies inside me.

I stormed on to the ward screaming and was immediately seen to by a full floor of staff, who plonked me in a wheelchair and showed me to my room.

Bill, who was ten minutes behind me, said that when the elevator doors opened, all he could hear was me screaming and he was worried I wouldn't hold on for my planned C-section. He raced to my side at the same time my doctor arrived. Everyone was concerned since my last labour was quick. The doctor walked in, put on a glove and shoved his entire arm up my clacker to see how many centimetres dilated I was.

There was an awkward silence.

Now I have never actually been fisted, it's just not a road I've been drawn to travel during my sexual escapades. Despite extreme disappointment on many a penis size, I still never went the full fist. Until now ... And I gotta say, momentarily it snapped me out of labour pain.

I'm kidding, it was shit. I don't recommend the fist.

And it became even more shit when the doctor ended his silence with: "Constance, you're not even one centimetre dilated?" He looked genuinely confused about my non-existent pain threshold.

Crappiest first fist ever.

Oh well, I guess none of us wants to see what will happen if I get to ten centimetres then, do we? Hurry up and give me my DRUGS!!!

Within half an hour, I was being wheeled into my glorious C-section like the fertility Queen that I am.

The definition of giving birth is "the act or extraction of a foetus and its membranes". So just to clarify, if you have had a C-section, you have still "given birth". Bravo, you rule.

You're allowed to have a plan, you're allowed to not have a plan, you're allowed to have a plan and change your mind, you're allowed to feel disappointed and you're allowed to be immensely proud of yourself. There are no rules.

Most of us have a little bit of every typecast inside us, some are the quintessential stereotypical one-way birthers. And some of us are even lucky enough to have a birth go to plan from start to finish.

One thing we all have in common is that we are women who want the absolute best for our little purple aliens, at whatever cost. We just want safe arrivals and I think that unites us all.

There is only one piece of unasked-for advice that I like to shove down every pregnant woman's throat:

Do NOT ever let anyone else persuade you to give birth the way THEY think is right, this is your journey.

I don't care if all the hipsters are squeezing them out in the VIP section of a new bar on opening night. I'm not.

You are entitled to feel disappointed in the way things happen but you're not allowed to feel disappointed in yourself. Ever.

Sorry, bitches, that's a rule and the only result that I will not allow.

You could be just like me and expect very little of yourself — that's really helpful. While being wheeled out of my C-section, I was quoted saying to the surgeon, "Fuck, I'm incredible, did you see what I just did?"

Never a disappointment, always a fucking hero.

CHAPTER 2
The Baby is Out

Many women feel like there is nothing more magical than that moment when you meet your baby. They look up at you all full of wonder, so innocent, so delicious, so much a part of you. The bond is instant, your fierce lioness mothering warrior exposes herself the moment you lock eyes. BONDED.

"I love you so, so, so much (sniffs, kisses, sniffs). You're all mine, forever and ever."

And then there are those who have the baby, look at it and say: "Oh look at you. Very cute, but … you look kind of lost mate, where are you off to? I'll get someone to give you a lift."

I'm somewhere in-between, I never got that magic rush of hormonal obsession with my babies. I think it came over a few months. I was, however, straight away very protective and certain that I knew best.

I've always wanted the absolute best for my babies. I just didn't necessarily need to be the one to give it to them. If a midwife wanted to take one for a few hours, I was already curled up asleep before she had gotten out the door.

Exhaustion plays a huge factor. When you have a traumatic labour that lasts for hours and then straight away begin the intense learning curve that is breastfeeding, without so much as a chance to catch your breath and give yourself a 'fuck me dead, wtf just happened?' moment, you're bound to be in a little shock.

Excitement, love, still drugged off your head and in shock.

And that's OK, it is totally understandable to be in complete and utter shock over what you have gone through.

That's just kind of the way we are set up in our culture. I know you have twenty-five stitches in your fanny or tummy, you have a catheter in (which is amazing by the way, after getting up every four minutes to wee for the last month of your pregnancy, nothing says relax quite like being able to lie there and piss yourself all night, I cried when mine was taken out), your milk hasn't come in yet and there is still a needle in your spine. But here's your baby, good luck doll ... Byyyyyyyyyyeee.

And BAM, you're a mum. You have something huge to live for, to succeed for, to be judged on, that you would actually die for. Daunting, right?

You need to be prepared for this shit.

LIMIT YOUR VISITORS

Not by numbers — feel free to have an army of Queens to the rescue — but by quality. The people who visit you in hospital at this point must fit strict criteria. Right now, you, my Queen, are at your absolute most exposed and vulnerable.

Everyone who walks through that door into the hospital room must be someone you are happy to …

1. Fumble around trying to learn how to breastfeed in front of. It's tough mastering breastfeeding — how to hold the baby, teaching the baby how to attach etc. You can get really frustrated and anybody who's been in the same room as me while I tried to sew will tell you, frustrated women can be real arseholes, which brings me to point two.

2. Yell at. If you have been trying to get a baby to attach and get some milk so it might actually do the one thing that you haven't done in two days and sleep, and someone is there trying to tell you what you're doing wrong, be prepared. You're going to yell at them.

3. Tell to fuck off. People are lovely, they love newbies. I remember being so pleasantly surprised when I had my first baby and saw how many people were attracted to babies. They are little cuddle magnets, it's really special. If you are feeling lonely, you can just stroll down to the shops with one and everyone starts talking to you. However, some people outstay their welcome. My long-time friend from high school came to visit me the day I had Arlo and just didn't leave. He ate my hospital meal, tried to steal my painkillers and pretended to the nurses that he was the dad when Bill went out to take a call. Now I could have told him to fuck off. I didn't because he's a funny bastard but the point is I could have, so he meets my criteria. The last thing you want to do post-birth is wait politely for some baby creep to get the message that they are outstaying their welcome.

4. Show your bits to. Nipples look funny when they're in a breast pump, getting sucked through the cylinder repetitively. Not for everyone. Then the midwife walks in and asks you if she can check your sanitary pad to monitor your blood loss. Does your husband's aunty's hairdresser's uncle need to see the chunky bloody afterbirth coming out of your mangled vagina? Nope.

5. Cry in front of. Word of warning: you will cry and cry and cry. It's not even depressing crying, it's more of a release. Women need emotional releases, we need a release after our favourite Bachelorette gets the boot instead of a rose so you can only imagine the release you'll need after a nine-month pregnancy, giving birth, not sleeping and your first few days of motherhood. The floodgates are open, only let in those who are prepared because there is no holding that shit in.

I am far from saying be alone. Do not be alone, be selective. Some of my favourite memories are of me and my closest, dearest friends in my hospital room. I was angry at Bill so when the girls came in, one holding the baby, one holding my nipple steady for the breast pump so that I could have a moment alone with my iPhone, I felt truly contented. They are my army of fresh air.

There will be pressure, your partner may insist that his family gets to come and see the baby. I totally understand why even a Queen like yourself feels like she has to agree to this but be assertive and have a time limit. You are experiencing the biggest change in your adult life and you are vulnerable, no negativity allowed. Blame hospital staff, blame visiting hours, do whatever needs to be done to put your own needs first.

The hospital room is for two things:

1. Support. Anyone is welcome to tell you how fabulous you are, to remind you of how beautiful you are, to blow-dry your hair, to hold the baby while you sleep, to get some really good photos for Facebook.

2. To make you laugh. Anyone who has a natural ability to see the humour in everything gets a red-carpet welcome to your hospital room. End of.

DON'T TAKE MIDWIVES TOO PERSONALLY

Like any occupation, in the world of midwifery you get a wide range of personalities. Some feel like a long-lost aunty with golden rays of invaluable advice, while others are quite simply plain nasty.

You will get separation anxiety from some when they knock off and you will creepily count down the hours until they return. With others you'll be tempted to lodge a request that they never be allowed to step foot in your room again.

On the day of my C-section, in the private hospital that I had pretended to be a posh bitch to get into, I was lying on the bed, still in a drug coma. The twins were in the nursery getting monitored and Bill was standing by my bed updating me on them when a midwife walked in to check my stats, including having a look at my pad for blood loss.

Bill made some polite chitchat with her, found out where she was from (Bill must get to the bottom of every single accent he hears) and formed what I thought was a pretty good rapport.

Now I can be a bit of a think-out-loud, no-filter kind of gal, so I tend to respond with compassion when a fellow female makes the same mistake around me. Which probably explains why at the time I didn't get too mad when this particular midwife pulled down my undies, checked my pad and then said out loud "oh yuck!"

I know! I can imagine it wasn't the prettiest sight, a bit of blood, tangled in pubes. Remember I wasn't expecting to have the babies for another week and being pregnant with twins, I could barely wipe my own arse, let alone shave my minge. But I could think of a million professional ways to describe it that didn't incorporate the word YUCK. Why even describe it at all?

What made it worse is that she looked so genuinely shocked and disappointed with herself that the words slipped out. She immediately apologised, me and Bill looked at each other, kind of in shock, and then we lost it laughing.

Looking back the whole thing was pretty odd. She was definitely one of those midwives whose face I was happy to never see again.

LET THE TEARS FLOW
Fuck the baby blues.

I totally get it, every time I get it. Whether it's crying in the shower or crying myself to sleep or crying when Bill goes back to work, I get it. I am a crier anyway so postpartum tears are not a surprise. Who wouldn't cry?

What I don't like is the term "baby blues" because it freaks me out — that impending doom that hits a few days after giving birth.

I get anxious waiting for the blues. There is nothing jazzy nor rock'n'roll about these blues.

To me, the baby blues is more a release — of hormones, anxiety and built-up frustrations. I love a good release, it feels so relieving to get it out after being strong for so long. You know how people say "Don't watch that movie or listen to that album, it's really sad and will make you cry?" Well, that doesn't freak me out, I look forward to that because I know I need a good cry and it can uplift me.

Don't fear the release and don't hold it in, let it out like a stunning wave of emotion. There is no better therapy than a good cry. At such an emotional and overwhelming time in your life, the most important thing you can do is embrace the release and let it go.

I always get two bouts of the release. One at the hospital, from the exhaustion and disappointment. (Bill is disappointing after I've given birth, I should be used to it and not let him come but every time I have expected more and gotten less … Men.) And then when I get home, because after three days of looking forward to coming home, thinking things will be so much better once you get there, the reality can be disheartening to say the least.

Cry — it's what sets us apart from men, we are so emotionally connected and in tune with ourselves. Cry and enjoy it.

AFTER BIRTH POO

As if having nurses poke and prod at your boobs every three hours, having a little bundle of foreignness wrapped up in a bassinet and still being in agony from your C-section or vag birth aren't enough to bring on the baby blues, along comes your first ABP or "After Birth Poo". I believe it is possibly more painful than your actual labour.

If recovering from a vag birth, pushing is out of the question. It will only bring back bad memories, you have seriously pushed enough for years worth of pooing. Your muscles are bruised and if you tore or were cut, your bum is now way closer to your vagina than ever before. I recommend waiting until your poo is so ready, it comes without any pushing, like it has its own little motor to hoon down your bowels and plop out.

If recovering from a C-section, you will run into other problems. After mine, I was offered laxatives. Why the fuck didn't I take them? For some strange medical reason, I had midwives asking me every hour if I had farted yet. It doesn't matter how many stitches and catheters have gone into your vagina, when a straight-faced midwife asks you if you have farted in the last hour, you always do your embarrassed laugh.

If the answer is "no", they don't let you eat a proper meal, if it's yes, they do.

Honestly, I thought I was being punked and was getting excited about the idea of Ashton Kutcher appearing from behind a curtain with his camera crew to discuss my post-surgery fart. Apparently "I know you're there, Ashton" wasn't the fart answer my nurses were looking for.

Back to the poo, I was certainly kicking myself in a few days when my ABP was still MIA. Finally, a nurse convinced me to take the laxative. Thank god I did.

The painkillers I'd had for the surgery backed me up completely, the turd that was waiting for me was humungous. You know how women gather around each other to brag about whose baby was bigger: "Mine was 4.2 kilos and let me tell you ladies, I pushed her out with no pain relief and a two-hour labour, thank you very much."

Well, I was looking for a mothers' congregation to have a similar conversation about my ABP, never found one so I'll just have it with you now. Seriously, it had to have been at least a kilo and yes, no pain relief. I do not know why we aren't allowed to keep our epidural in at least until we get the first turd out because good grief … it's not easy.

Now I'm going to be completely honest here — seriously only Bill, my mum and my sister know about this — my ABP was so big that it gave me an anal fissure (sounds kind of French, doesn't feel French), which is a small tear on your anus. The problem is that we need to eat to live, and eating means pooing, which re-opens the tear. So I was in agony for every poo for months. Bill would say "what's wrong?" and I would reply with "I have to poo. I've quit smoking, drinking, I never see my friends, I don't sleep. Pooing was the last thing I had in my life that I enjoyed. It was my 'me time'. Only now it hurts like a motherfucker, I fear it, I feel like I've lost a piece of me."

Bill was really sad for me.

Eventually, my anal fissure healed — au revoir fissure — but please Queens, if you ever listen to anything that I have to share: TAKE THE LAXATIVES.

After my ABP release, my hormonal and emotional release, and having a militant feeding/sleeping routine shoved down my throat, I'm usually quite ready to go home.

CHAPTER 3
Homecoming

The parental guilt of having more than one child is strong, it hits you like a brick wall. Arlo was my easiest labour, a plump, healthy baby along with a minimal-damage delivery, so I was ready to go home the next day. Because Arlo wasn't my first, I had my first true love in the form of the cutest little girl waiting for me at home.

When my mum brought Billie-Violet in to meet her new brother at the hospital, I was ready. I had been advised to have a photo of her next to the baby's bassinet, not just for my benefit but also so that she would see it when she walked in and feel like she was still right in the middle of her family and not by any means shoved to the side.

Of course the sentiment was completely lost on her, she didn't even notice.

Two-year-old Billie-Violet did the mandatory pose holding the baby so I could post the picture on Facebook and everyone could comment about how they had such a powerful bond and I could pat myself on the back for being a great mum etc etc. Then big sis dropped the baby on the bed, gave me a sympathy hug and skipped out the door with her grandma who had promised her a trip to the toy shop. Her developmentally appropriate narcissism was in full swing.

How can children be so sensitive yet so resilient at the same time?

Some women want to go home as soon as possible while others want to milk it (literally) and stay in hospital until they are dragged out by security.

I was a go-home straightaway type of girl. I remember once trying to go downstairs for a coffee with my baby and being stopped by a militant nurse grabbing Arlo out of my arms and telling me it was against hospital regulations to let me off the ward with my baby.

I totally understand this, if they didn't have rules like this any old Jo could be kidnapping drugged-up mums' babies while they recovered, however when you're as anti-establishment and opposed to authority as I am, having someone try to take your baby from you is enough to get your bags packed.

I went home that day.

Home to my glorious little Queen of Rad-ness, to be abused and treated like shit in general for daring to cheat on her with this new baby. As soon as we pulled up outside, Billie-Violet said: "Let's go inside mum, and dad can take Arlo back to the hospital so he can find his own family, poor baby Arlo."

Dividing my time between my new baby and my toddler was yet another thing to feel guilty about, as if I didn't already have enough things to loathe myself over.

Billie-Violet had gone two and a half years alone, with me as her only real friend. Now I was starting to feel like the rock that crumbled underneath her. Every single tantrum was a reminder to put aside a therapy fund for my abandoned little princess.

I was advised once by a GP to make sure that when I am finished feeding or changing a nappy to tell the baby (even though he can't understand a goddamn thing I say) that it is Billie-Violet's turn for some mum time now and he needs to wait. Obviously this serves no purpose at all for the baby but is a sweet reminder to your child that the baby has to make sacrifices too. I don't know whether I was told this as a way of reassuring my daughter or a way of calming my own guilt. I think both are as important as each other.

The night that I brought the twins home after my C-section was an all-time low. Bill and I were barely talking at that point in our relationship. He had arranged to meet some mutual friends for dinner, not knowing that the doctors would discharge (that word along with moist has been ruined by vaginas) me a couple of days early. I called him, he picked me up and I didn't even complain about his decision to keep his plans and go out to dinner. Everything was fine, over the last couple of days with a bit of practice I had figured out a way that I could hold a baby and carefully manage to not pop a stitch as I moved. That was it though, anything heavier or if I laughed or coughed …
BAM, stitches popped, intestines out and all over the floor in front of me. Pleasantly surprised at how easy my recovery was, Bill went out and I had the kids.

All was going well until my now three-year-old Arlo was having a bath with Billie-Violet. At the end when the plug was pulled, he went to get out and grab the red towel. But his cunning big sister, who's always on the lookout for ways to mess with him, swiped it first. Arlo lost his shit and, insulted by my offering of the green towel, snatched it off me and threw it aside, sitting on his wet bum. I grabbed the red towel off Billie-Violet and tried to wrap up Arlo. But it was too late, he was absolutely beside himself with fury that Billie-Violet had the audacity to take the red towel knowing full well that he was reaching for it.

I needed to snap Arlo out of this as the twins were asleep, which gave me roughly half an hour before one of them would wake up and I so needed this thirty minutes for myself. I know there is only one way to snap Arlo out of one of these meltdowns and that is to bend down, scoop him up and soothe his tears while he sobs in my arms.

Even though my tummy ached, it was worth it. And rather than hating Arlo or my life, I did the natural thing and hated Bill.

He came home at 10pm, half drunk and really happy. He whispered through the closed door of the room, "I've had an amazing night" and asked how I was. I couldn't reply, instead feeling around for something to grab. I threw an Ugg boot at the door and Bill went off to his bed.

The most important thing you need to remind yourself is that you are doing this for your kids. Surely the only reason we have more than one is to keep the others company. I mean you don't even realise how easy one kid is until you have another and then another. By then you envy people with one child for their relaxing lives. But you had more than one to keep your little love cub company in this world, that fact alone needs to relieve you of any guilt you're feeling over a two-year-old throwing herself on the floor, screaming her little head off because you are no longer singing her fourteen songs and reading her a dozen books before bed. Dry your eyes little turd, you have a sibling.

PRECIOUS LITTLE SUCKLING MONSTERS

Feeding a baby is so easy, it's so natural, there is no rule book because we don't need one. It just happens. That's what you hear when the baby is still in your belly.

Once the little one's out, you're playing a whole new ball game. With no rules, or rules that change every day, or rules that have their own list of exceptions that can be overturned by an emergency at any time.

Confused?

Welcome to Breastfeeding.

Breastfeeding is not the peaches and cream, blow-dried hair, fluffy baby, softly lit image that pro-breast activists will have you believe. Now don't get me wrong, I did enjoy a long slog of breastfeeding Billie-Violet and Arlo. I'm just a realist. In the beginning, it's fucking tough.

I have naturally huge tits, they sagged from a very young age. In fact, they grew saggy — I was an eleven-year-old with saggy tits. I'm OK with it, however when my milk finally came in — and every time it felt like it took forever — boy did they fill up. I felt like a porn star, I felt like an OHS hazard, I was worried that the male hospital staff would lose balance due to their massive stiffies after laying eyes on old porno tits over here.

Along with these rock-solid Baywatch beauties comes great pain. In fact, friends who have had implants once their breastfeeding days were over have told me that the pain of the implant was nothing compared to the pain of their milk coming in. So when you do lay eyes on that advertising campaign of the mum with her perfect blow-dry whose baby so naturally suckles on her breast while she lovingly gazes at him with a smile, know that underneath that smile the words "I wish these arseholes with their cameras would politely fuck right off and let me go back to screaming this motherfucking house down".

Cracked nipples sting. Some women will tell you that if your nipples are bleeding and cracked, your baby isn't latching properly. Well, I'm here to tell you that all nipples crack and hurt, not just those of us who struggle with baby-latching scenarios. I'd like to officially thank those women who are like ninjas waiting in the shadows for something to go wrong so that they can karate ninja chop out of their hiding places to tell us what big fucking failures we are.

I have never had an issue with breastfeeding in public. I love tits, big ones, little ones, saggy ones, perky ones and ones full of milk make my heart sing sha-lala-lala-la-la. I'm that creepy chick who's intently staring and smiling at you while you're breastfeeding, then starts lactating as you reach for your phone to call in back-up.

So you can only imagine that when I was breastfeeding, I was super proud. I would pull them out everywhere, nowhere was off-limits. At the pub, boobs out, at the hairdresser's, boobs out — I even walk fed. People sometimes stared at the walk feed, obviously admiring me and my legendary multi-tasking abilities.

I spent nearly five years breastfeeding. By the end you get so comfy that when your toddler walks up to you at a restaurant and pulls down your top to have a suck, you continue chatting to your mates. Even after toddler walks off, it's a good five minutes before you realise that your boobs are still out, no baby attached. Your mates are so used to your tits that they didn't even notice either until the waitress arrives with your dinner and awkwardly states: "Here's your fish and tits ... I mean fish and chips .... not tits ... you have the tits, I just have chips."

I have been waiting all these years for someone to have a go at me for breastfeeding in public, I have so many comebacks that I'm just dying to respond with, but would you believe that I have never once been criticised for it? It's always the way! I'm caught off-guard every day and abused for bad driving, bad parenting, bad kids, bad parking or pushing in at the bank but never once have I been breastfeeding shamed. Which I suppose is a great thing, it means folks are finally getting it, that it's natural and part of life, tits are glorious — they should be free! Only I can't help but feel a little disappointed, it would have been grand to let out some of my anger on someone who wasn't poor old Bill.

Breastfeeding gets easier, less mechanical, more enjoyable and relaxing all the time. When your baby is holding itself up and helping itself to your boob, it's definitely a more relaxing job. I'm not going to lie, sometimes when that baby of yours is falling asleep on your boob, eyes rolling back like a junkie, you too can fall into an endorphin-filled state of bliss. Nothing beats it.

There is no set time to feed until. For me with Billie-Violet and Arlo, I had wanted to get to six months and ended up getting to nearly two years until I decided that I wanted my body back. There is still a stigma attached to women who breastfeed long term — people tend to comment negatively when a woman is nursing a child who walks and talks. I say fuck them. Queens support other women whether they decide to formula feed from the beginning or breastfeed long term (I'm not endorsing being that creepy bitch who visits her son at uni and peels him off his new girlfriend for some booby) but we Queens are an all-inclusive sisterhood.

49

Breastfeeding isn't for everyone. Sometimes the cracked nipples, unsettled baby and stench of sour milk just isn't worth it. That's cool too.

My twins self-weaned when they were about six months old. I acted all shocked but secretly I knew it came down to the fact that every second feed I was giving them formula. Turns out they are piglets like their mumma and wanted the faster, more filling option.

What a relief formula was for me. I had felt like I was teetering on a fence for six months, on one side of the fence I could see my happy place — content babies, a husband I didn't want to smother in his sleep and me being glamorous. On the other side, I saw a broken marriage, miserable kids and me chugging down Valium with a bottle of vodka. I felt like I was walking the thin line between postnatal depression and coping. Once I switched to formula, I finally jumped off the fence and landed on my happy side.

I don't know if that relief came from the ease of the physical burden — having to feed two babies all the time and having my nutrition sucked out of me — or if it was more of a subconscious, psychological thing. Knowing that we can leave our babies and they will be OK, is sometimes all we need to regain sanity. I'm guessing for me, it was a mixture of both things. It definitely had a huge effect on my happiness.

Queens don't fail at anything, they learn lessons and they change their minds.

That goes for breastfeeding as well. We all have our limits, the real skill is in knowing our limits. If breastfeeding is pushing you to yours, jump on the happy side of the fence. Going from being a breast mum to a formula mum, I can tell you, without a doubt in my mind, that your bond with your baby is not at risk at all.

Breast or formula, you are mum, you are the hero. I've said it before and I'll say it again, Queenies' sanity comes first.

MEN WHEN YOU BRING HOME BABY

Taking your baby home is one of the scariest things you will ever do. I don't care if you're on baby number one or baby number eleven, there will be a whole lot of "what the fucks?" coming out of a whole lot of mums' mouths at this time in their lives.

Women have so many jobs — push the baby out … learn to feed it … look after your birth wounds … get some sleep… but don't sleep too heavily and don't stress out, it will stop your milk supply.

Men have one job — install the fucking car seat. And do you think that on our third and fourth baby, Bill could get his head around a properly installed baby seat in time for me returning home from hospital?

I could go on and on about the holy fucking letdown disaster that is a new dad. I try to remain compassionate, I try to keep an open mind, I really do, but I find it increasingly difficult when one can't even install one's baby seat into the car even though one had forty weeks notice.

Not all men are as useful as a spare dick when you bring home a baby. I hear old wives' tales about this guy who did night feeds and changed shitty nappies and learnt how to bath the baby and did basically everything with the older kids but I have never actually met anyone who knew him … and boy did I search.

I do actually have one friend with that perfect guy. He couldn't be more involved, in fact he almost annoys her by striving to be so supportive. And she loves him, really loves him. Even when she brought home the baby, she still loved him, it was so strange. Before they had children, I was that smug bitch sitting back, gleefully telling her to "get back to me once you've had a kid with him, then tell me he's still a hero". Only now they have popped out three and he is still a winner, so helpful and respectful. The rest of us gather around her asking for more stories of this godly creature. I don't know if I'm intrigued and in awe of her, if I find her "perfect" relationship so hard to relate to or if I'm creeped out by what a big fat liar she must be.

When Queens arrive home from hospital, there should be a red carpet lined by photographers while neighbours strum harps at your gate. Most of all, boyfriends and husbands should dedicate weeks to bending over backwards and attending to your every need.

Instead you seem to be greeted with screaming toddlers, piles of washing that wasn't done while you were in the hospital and your fella's mates who come over to meet the baby. Yet they walk straight past the bassinet without even peering in and over to the beer fridge. Disappointing.

If I ever got pregnant again, which I won't because Bill has had the snip and neither of us have the strength for another baby, but if I did, I wholeheartedly swear I would make Bill move out for a month. He would be obliged to take the other children with him too because being up with a screaming baby all night, every night is hard enough without the knowledge that the man who did this to you has his feet up, is drunk or playing Angry Birds on his phone. Unbearable.

KNOCK AND RUN
Queens need each other. If you put too many expectations on your husband, your frustration levels go through the roof. Call a Queen instead. They understand. You may need help babysitting the other kids or doing

the school run or you need food and supplies dropped off outside your front door, like a knock and run, only with delicious homemade dinners instead of a dog poo in a paper bag on fire.

Any friend who has brought home a baby knows the power of the knock and run. Sometimes a Queen can't stand the idea of being face to face with anyone, 24/7 of feeding, pumping, crying, not sleeping, fighting with your husband, parental guilt … It just goes on and on and on. You're allowed to not want to see anyone, yet you need help. Knock and run. Get your number one Queenie Bee to work out a roster of knock and runs that lasts a week or two — you should be ready to open the blinds and re-enter the world after that. Take your time, Queens need time, but monitor yourself. Don't isolate yourself too much or you might start to get used to it and then it will only get harder to re-enter the real world.

The first few weeks are an absolute balancing act but you can do it, you're a Queen.

The bright side is that you have a baby and when it's not screaming or waking you up, it's actually really cute. You have an overwhelming need to protect and care for the little wrapped-up worm and you deserve every droplet of love that pours out of its head when it looks up at you.

The negative is that this is the hardest time in your life to hold on to your Queenhood. You can feel it slip further and further away. The secret that took me four kids to learn? It actually never goes anywhere, you just can't feel it for a while. You can't see your crown but trust me Queenie, it's there, stronger than ever.

While your Queenhood may be lying dormant, it is in fact gaining momentum, ready for you to shine the fuck out of that crown.

When one of my friends is having a shit day with a new baby, I like to tell them my rock-bottom story, because no matter how shit your day is, it's not usually as shit as this.

The worst "not coping, fuck my life" day that I can remember was the day the twins had to get an ultrasound on their hips at six weeks old.

I had Arlo with us as well. Nobody could help. Bill and my mum had to work and I was so determined not to look like I "couldn't cope" that I didn't call anyone else.

I parked at the hospital and for some reason I thought that putting one twin in the baby carrier and holding the other was easier than putting them in the pram.

I lined up in a massive queue at the ultrasound place, the twins started squawking so I was jiggling them to keep them happy.

Arlo was in and out of my sight, annoying elderly people and climbing on chairs.

Twins' squawking became screams, my jiggles became full-blown star jumps to entertain them.

The nurse asked if we could wait in a hospital bay, probably so that Arlo would stop trying to mug patients on their way in.

We did so.

After an hour we were called into the longest ultrasound of our lives.

Both twins' hips were fine.

We had to line up to pay, the twins screaming again.

Arlo collapsed next to a vending machine in desperate need of a lemonade, I couldn't even reach my purse.

The Queen behind the counter told me she'd email me the bill.

Thank fuck.

Arlo still lying down in lemonade protest,

I step over him.

The pitch of the twins' scream sends a shiver up my spine and I feel like

I'm about to lose my shit at the world.

Instead I breathe and somehow convince Arlo to come with me to the car.

The sun is beaming on the twins' little heads, I get panicked, skin cancer ads floating around my head.

I swiftly get to the car, guiding Arlo out of oncoming traffic by screaming because I have no free hands, everyone's staring.

I get to the car, it's boiling hot, the twins are screaming and going red, I realise I haven't paid for my parking ticket.

I yell for Arlo to follow me, we need to find the parking pay station, he bursts into tears and yells that he wants a lemonade.

I feel that anxiety creeping up again and look everywhere, with three screaming humans attached to me,

I can't find it anywhere so I walk back to the car.

The kids are roasting, I need to get them in the air-conditioning. I start the car and get everyone in.

There is no way I'm getting everyone out again to find the pay station. I drive to the boom gate and shove my unpaid ticket in,

It doesn't open.

Someone says something in the intercom, I offer my credit card details but he says no. "Pay for your ticket."

Cars pile up behind me, beeping at me, someone gets out of their car and walks towards me,

I wind up my window and lock my door, look straight ahead and burst into tears. Security comes,

Asks me why I didn't pay for my ticket.

I explain to him that the pay station was hidden or camouflaged and my three children could have the beginning stages of melanoma after looking for it.

I offered to pay him, He said no,

I wound up the window again and called my mum crying.

By now there were eight cars behind me beeping and three drivers standing by my car.

My mum told me to put her on to the security guard,

I unwound my window a bit and held up my phone on loudspeaker. My mum gave him a mouthful, he agreed I could just pay him.

I was $2 short, I told him I had a credit card,

He shook his head and the boom gates opened,

I nearly crashed into an ambulance on my way out.

Drove to the nearest takeaway and got Arlo a massive lemonade. Called my mum and somehow we both laughed,

The end.

Moral of the story, we all have really fucked days, sometimes the only option is to laugh at yourself.

There is a good old eastern mantra, "This too shall pass". There aren't any simple answers to how to get through this time, except this: there is nothing at all wrong with you for struggling through the first few months. Everyone does, and anyone who claims to find it easy should be kept at arms' length and approached with caution or should be sharing their drugs.

It gets better — every week, every month gets easier. You get a little more sleep, your baby gets a little more independent. Before you know it, you're waking up from a five-hour sleep stint, popping her on a playmat where she entertains herself for twenty minutes while you drink a cup of tea and shave your legs, sanity regained. You just have to hold on tight because This Too Shall Pass.

SLEEPING, WHAT THE FUCK IS THAT?

Babies don't know how to sleep without you. That is a simple fact, they do learn but it's a very foreign concept to a squawky little love cub.

Can we blame them? I don't like sleeping alone and I'm thirty-three. Nights are still a scary world out there if I'm alone. Bill, on the other hand, likes being alone, he pretends he's off to the toilet and instead sneaks on to the couch and within fifteen seconds he's snoring. So annoying. Thankfully I have had four babies so I never have to be alone again.

I know a couple of Queens who are totally cool with sleep deprivation, they just float through the days accepting it and look fine and seem to cope.

Me? I absolutely fall apart. I cry my eyes out, I rock in the corner facing the wall, I call my mum in tears and threaten Bill about filing for divorce. By the third time I am woken up in the middle of the night, my body physically reacts. I get a migraine and feel like I'm about to vomit. Seriously, two night feeds are my absolute limit.

None of my babies have been natural-born sleepers but what is a natural-born sleeper? A baby with a mum who's very good at applying make-up and concealing her insanity? I have been told that I "catastrophise" lack of sleep. Um catastrophise? It is a fucking catastrophe, what could be more of an emergency than not sleeping. It is used as a form of torture. And now you are being tortured relentlessly. That sounds more like a catastrophe and less like me being a drama Queen if you ask me.

What even the fuck is sleep? Oh it's that thing that your boyfriend does all night while you stay up with a screaming baby, that teases you every now and then with twenty minutes rest, only to wait until that deep realm kicks in and bam you're up again. Good times.

I can't handle sleep deprivation. I just do not function, and if I can't function, I can't love. More than not being able to love properly, I turn into a full-blown irrational arsehole. I remember being so sleep deprived with my first baby that I began fantasising about getting a nanny to do night shifts. Of course I couldn't afford a nanny so I fantasised about robbing a bank or shop to pay my nanny cash. Then I thought to myself that if I got caught, I'd go to jail, but hey, at least I'd be able to sleep a full night. So there I was fantasising about going to jail because that would be a better option than one more broken night's sleep with my newborn.

There is no time to recover from childbirth, realistically you should get a month of being fed grapes by a topless Greek man, but somehow you end up going home with your old boyfriend who still thinks that the baby's attached to you. It's not, you wish it was, you spend your nights imagining that you're a kangaroo and have a pouch that you could pop your baby in to get some rest. Ironically, this fantasy kind of sounds a bit like pregnancy, with your baby inside your tummy, which of course you hated too. Cue the "maybe it's me" lightbulb moment. Fuck off, it's not you. It really is a shit time.

They say sleep when they sleep … bahahahhahah. Have you ever heard more crock of shit from someone who clearly has never permanently looked after a newborn in their lives! Let alone a newbie with older siblings or a twin.

Even with just one newborn, they fall asleep in your arms and if by some weird stroke of luck, the baby miraculously stays asleep when you put it into the cot, how do you want to celebrate? With a nap? The first moment you have had to yourself all day, a moment that could last three minutes or could last an hour and you are supposed to have a nap?

Fuck no!! You're gonna walk over to that little bitch of a kettle that you've been looking at all day and if your baby is still asleep when it's boiled, the badass inside you will sit on your still-padded-from-pregnancy arse and not only drink a cup of tea but … you guessed it … grab your iPhone and have that Facebook stalk, make that call, look at Instagram, read the news or just take a goddamn selfie to look back on and remember this fine moment. The moment you had no baby in your arms and you drank a goddamn cup of tea. Because that, my friends, is all I ever wanted when I had a newborn, ten minutes to myself for a cup of tea.

So think about that MEN, when you march in after a day's work with your holier-than-thou attitude and a look that is giving off the good old "what have you done all day?" vibe. Think about me, sitting on the couch giving my kettle seductive looks and getting tingly clitoral sensations over ten fucking minutes alone with my tea.

You don't necessarily learn how to get babies into good sleep routines just because you have had four babies. What you do learn, however, is to not stress about it too much. I suppose you learn that there isn't really much you can do about it other than wait, and that they do get better.

I have learnt to stick, more or less, to these guidelines. They seem to help me direct my babies into some kind of a sleep pattern. If I ever have another baby (God forbid), I would do this from the beginning.

1. I don't feed my babies breast milk or formula between the hours of 4pm and 6pm (or whatever works for you and your fella as a suitable time to put them to bed). Most of the other times of the day, I'm a demand feeder. Midwives tried to get me into a routine of only feeding them every three or four hours and I usually failed miserably at that. I can't help feeding their squawky little mouths when I know it will comfort them. However, when 4pm arrives and I can see the light of a 6 o'clock bed time, I play hard ball. So I distract them the following ways: walk them around the house, go outside for a nice breeze blowing through their three strands of hair, bath time, whatever it takes.

Then come 6pm, they are hungry enough to take a huge feed which will hopefully get them to sleep for a bit longer than usual and you get your evening break. I find the day so much easier to get though if I know the Queen gets a break at six.

2. I don't bring them out of their room after their 6pm bedtime

and I don't turn the light on when I go in there. Babies don't know the difference between day and night, they have no idea that they are supposed to be awake during the day and asleep during the night. It is up to us to teach them. I have always told Bill or anyone else who's babysitting for me that unless there is something wrong, leave them in their rooms. Go in to feed or cuddle them or rock them to sleep but keep it dark in there. That way they can associate darkness with sleeping and slowly, gently nudge them into some sort of routine. Of course if they are sick or have had a bad dream or if you are sensing something isn't quite right, then turn on the light or carry the cherub into the lounge room. But as a general rule, I have been known to dive at someone who goes into my babies' room to get them out — in slow motion saying "noooooooooooooooooooo".

I remember getting a knock at the door after I had Billie-Violet, she had only been home from the hospital for a week. Bill was still pretty clueless as to what my new "role" was. I think it's easy for someone to assume that when you bring a baby home, you will now be the one to look after all the housework and baby and cooking while they work and bring in the cash.

Of course fine sir, would you also like a beer and blow job on arrival?

Wouldn't that be lovely and maybe it works for some, it does not work for me. I am the first Queen to put up my hand and say "I don't want to!" and even if I did, "Is that even possible?" For the first few weeks, definitely not.

Something has to go, I usually chose housework, then cooking and finally I call someone to look after the baby too. That's what happens when I'm pushed to do too much — I do nothing.

So on this particular day, I answered the door and I saw my absolutely beautiful friend Jess standing there, holding homemade food with a huge warm smile on her face. Do you know how I reacted? I burst into tears, I was so overwhelmed, so tired, I felt so much pressure to keep my shit together when my shit just wasn't together and my beautiful friend's kind face totally weakened me. She wasn't expecting that, she entered my fucked zone and saw how much help I needed.

Stacks of dishes, washing, baby crying, dog yapping, nappies everywhere, I was so overwhelmed. I hadn't slept, I stank of sour milk, I felt disgusting.

Jess put the food down and started cleaning the whole house while I breastfed and we both bitched about life. If only women could live with each other when we have babies, there ain't many problems in the world that can't be solved by a girlfriend who cleans your house and happily indulges a husband bitch sesh.

CONTROLLED CRYING, CO-SLEEPING

When Billie-Violet was born, everyone was talking about "cruel to be kind" routines. It was all the rage to leave a baby to cry it out, similar to the "controlled crying" method. I tried it a few times, it pulled on my heartstrings too much and gave me even greater anxiety so I sucked it up and accepted my sleep deprivation for a while longer.

Arlo was my creepy little co-sleeping, demand-fed baby. I think I was fancying myself as an Earth Mother for those few months. I booted Bill out of our bed and settled in nicely with my new man by my side.

I found rolling over to breastfeed him a hell of a lot easier than getting out of bed and sitting on a chair to feed, putting him back to bed and trying to get back to sleep myself.

A lot of people warned me that I could roll on him and suffocate him in my sleep but I was confident that he was safe. I didn't drink or smoke or take Valium at the time and was sleeping really lightly.

I planned to do the same with the twins but the reality was it didn't work out. I was too tired to sleep lightly. Having two of them was confusing me too much, with one on each side of me, I was worried that maybe I would roll on one when I woke up disorientated. I decided to put them back in their cots and slept next to them alone in my bed.

This was the most exhausted I have ever been in my life, some nights I was lucky to get thirty minutes sleep in between night feeds. One would wake and if I woke the other up to try to do both night feeds together, I would be up for almost an hour at a time. Bill was working a lot and was out first thing in the morning, leaving me alone to lug my sorry arse out of bed for school run.

I lasted eight months of this torture, I reread sleep books, I called a sleep school, nothing was helping. I was at my absolute wits' end and couldn't take it anymore. I couldn't be patient with my children, I couldn't be loving, I couldn't be me. So I made the painful decision to try "crying it out".

I moved my own sleeping HQ to sharing Arlo's bed and summoned all of the strength I could to prepare myself for a night of twins screaming the house down.

That is exactly what I got. Rumi woke up at midnight and began crying, my chest hurt and my eyes welled up, I could feel the abandonment that he was feeling. We were crying together, he cried for thirty minutes before his little soul realised for the first time in his life that mummy wasn't coming. He was almost asleep when his last little sob woke up Snow and the process started all over again with her screaming out for me, wanting comfort. I could hear her little voice change with despair when she worked out I wasn't coming. She slowly went from angry to sad to resigned to asleep.

My heart was shattered. I finally fell back to sleep, waiting for round two, which happened at 4am. The emotional rollercoaster of torture went on for two more nights yet by the third night they only woke up once and by the fourth night, they didn't wake up at all.

I have to say that as painful as hearing them cry was, it worked and from that day on, they have slept through, which means that I can love them with my whole heart, I can open my eyes in the morning, I can make breakfast, do school run, waste hours blowing raspberries on poking-out bellies.

The keyboard warriors and PPP (perfect parenting police) will try to convince you that controlled crying will lead to anxiety, and co-sleeping will put your baby at risk and that basically unless you are working your arse off and torturing yourself 24/7, you are not doing enough. But the truth is that you know your limits, pushing them will not benefit your baby. It will not make you some sort of hero, there is no cape waiting for you at the end of a sleepless night, there is just a really shitty day.

Do what you gotta do, Queenie, keeping your baby safe means keeping yourself safe. Get help, get advice and ignore the judgments.

There is a really serious side to sleep deprivation, terrible things can happen when a woman isn't getting enough sleep. I passionately believe it is the responsibility of the entire family to ensure that a mum is getting enough sleep.

New mums are relied on to make clear-headed decisions, decisions that impact the safety of their little baby. So many times I have caught myself doing something really weird due to sleep deprivation, from putting the remote control in the fridge to leaving my shopping in the trolley at the supermarket.

I understand that so many things contribute to "baby brain" — you have a lot on your mind as well as your hormones wreaking havoc. But exhaustion plays a huge role. I have been lucky, leaving my remote control in the fridge is just weird, not life changing. But what if that was a baby left in the car?

One time the twins fell asleep in the car and when I parked, I grabbed them out, put them in their cots, went straight to the couch and fell asleep. It's often 40 degrees in a Perth summer and when I woke up, I was really hot and sweaty. I turned on the air-conditioner and walked over to the windows to close them. My car caught my eye, it looked like a big black oven. Suddenly I felt a rush of panic, like I was about to vomit. I raced to the babies' room. Thankfully, my little angels were sleeping in their cots. But I can honestly tell you that at the time, I couldn't make out if moving them in there was a dream or not, I could barely remember doing it. What a scary thought. So tired.

I know that falling asleep on the couch while breastfeeding is incredibly dangerous and while I am a corner-cutting, relaxed type of mother, I have huge fears of cot death so I never did it.

But I have been sitting there, breastfeeding on the couch so tired that my eyelids felt like lead, using every inch of my strength to hold them up, knowing that my baby's safety relied on it. It was agony and had my subconscious not swiftly nudged me out of what was about to become a deep sleep, I could have unintentionally put my little cub in danger and I can tell you now, it is agony.

I can't help but feel resentful that if something did happen in either of these exhaustion-related scenarios, it would be me who would have to deal with it, me who would be on trial for neglect, me who wouldn't be able to live with myself for not being a "better" mum.

I don't believe that sleep deprivation should only be suffered by the primary caregiver. Just because we are staying at home with babies, why should we bear the entire brunt of sleepless nights?

Where is the logic in this? It's in the assumption that our job at home isn't as important as the income earner's, that we can handle being tired all day because we don't have to go to work. Well, the risks that you take going to work while tired are far less significant than the risks that you take being the sole carer of a baby while tired. I know I would prefer to lose my job than my child.

And that assumption that mums get to "sleep when the baby sleeps" — well you know what they say about assumptions, they make a fuckwit out of both of us.

In a perfect world, we wouldn't need to justify how difficult a day alone with a baby can be. In a perfect world, there wouldn't be a "whose day is harder" competition. In a perfect world, the sleep deprivation would be equally shared between both parents.

By the time your second, third, fourth or fifth babies come along, you're faced with the same old shit, just with a different baby. It may not necessarily get any easier but the agonising shock is gone and I have found comfort in the countdown.

You don't really get the countdown with your first, you're a rookie too busy stressing out over life. But when you've done it once, you develop that understanding that everything passes, that you won't be tired forever. So by the time you have your second baby, your entire life is counting down timeframes until it gets easier, like a light at the end of the tunnel.

Teaching a baby how to sleep can be lonely, relentless and depressing but is made bearable with snippets of golden moments. Babies are always at their cutest at 2am when they are desperately trying to get a rise out of you, it's almost like a secret love code that is only shared between the joyful little baby and the parent who could be bothered getting up to her. I will take those rewards any day.

Don't judge yourself for being a total fucking drama queen diva about it, you're absolutely entitled to it. Somewhere along the line in our culture, we were taught that we shouldn't complain about parenting, like it means that we aren't a "natural" if we find it hard. So we bottle everything up at the risk of looking like a failure and as a result we FEEL like royal failures, which is so much worse.

I believe I have complaining to thank for my sanity. Complaining and laughing. If you're over-tired and exhausted and think the world is full of arseholes, have a huge complain about it, followed by a laugh. Thank me later, Queenie.

WEANING
Bill and I went to Broome on our honeymoon. I thought this beautiful

coastal town in northern Western Australia was only for the rich and famous. But it turns out in the off-season it's for the average pleb too, simply because in summer it's a boob-sweat, vag-sweat that blends in with arse sweat, frizzy hair, totally sweltering place.

So naturally that makes even the most exclusive resorts half price and affordable to your average pleb. Like me and Bill.

I was still breastfeeding and really wanted to stop so that I could try to get pregnant again. (Yes, I am aware that I could still get pregnant while feeding, obviously I was kind of over having a toddler munch on my tits as well.) I had pretty severe anxiety over leaving Billie-Violet who at the time was eighteen months, torn between desperately wanting some time away from her at that demanding age and not ever wanting to leave her little side. We agreed on three nights in a Broome resort on our own.

Despite the vag-sweat, it was heaven. I didn't realise how desperately I needed time away from my daughter until I arrived there, the sweltering desert was my paradise, wine in the pool, delicious food, and me with my husband.

But then there was my tits. Weaning is painful, your tits start to fill up again like implants that leak milk. Two days in and I could no longer move. I was propped up in bed on my back but not fully on my back due to the rip I felt when they slipped into my armpits, yet not upright due to the rip that I would feel when I sat up. I tried milking myself in the shower, like a dairy farm cow, but I was having minimal success. I had no breast pump and was fantasising about my daughter emptying them for me. Every time I saw a toddler, I couldn't help but wonder if they would fancy some breast milk. I needed relief and suction was the only thing that would give it to me.

I don't mind a bit of a breast fondle, nipples aren't a bad weapon to use when seeking stimulation. I'm not opposed to the odd tongue-to-nipple arousal method when being a sex-goddess vixen. However … that all flies out the window the moment I conceive a baby. The moment a little soldier of sperm wins the battle and finds my glorious little egg, something in my nipples does a complete 180. They go from being a key participant in sexual stimulation to feeling like the equivalent of fingernail on blackboard. So having my boobs even looked at was like having the inside of my vagina painted with blackboard paint and then being fingered by Freddy Krueger. Nothing shrivels up my juices quite like it.

Luckily for me, Bill wasn't into breast milk … Sometimes I would squirt him with it, thinking that he would laugh and every single time he would get angry. I don't know if Bill was or wasn't breast fed, so I can't psychoanalyse where his repulsion came from but it suits me just fine, milky boobs are a no-go zone.

However, on this day, the day of boob pain and agony, feeling like I would explode, I swallowed my pride and turned to Bill. The only thing left to do was to get him to suck the milk out of my boobs.

He certainly didn't want to, the idea was violating him as much as it was violating me. Like two imprisoned strangers being forced to have sex for the entertainment of their captor.

I had to throw in the old "I'm in too much pain to go out tonight". Bill, of course, didn't want to stay home, he had the thirst. We both had the thirst, being child-free for the first time in a year and a half gives you the thirst.

There are no words to adequately describe the awkwardness of watching your husband drink from your breasts. I guess it was a "close your eyes and think of England" moment. Poor Bill was quivering while he covered my huge nipples with his goatee-enclosed mouth.

Those perfect soft suckling sounds that Billie-Violet had managed to melt me with were now the loud slurping sounds of a man trying to suck and hold back spew at the same time. He even threw in a burp. Kill me now.

This wasn't your average spit-or-swallow scenario so I reserved my rejection when he set up a little cup next to my tummy to spit the unloved milk into.

While Bill and I may have struggled to look at each other until our fifth drink that night, I like to look back at this as a bonding experience. It's always nice to know that your husband will go to any lengths to keep wifey out of pain.

Most Queens' first holiday away from her kids consists of crying on the flight there, not wanting to part with their little loves in case it severs some part of their bond, and then crying again on the flight home, struggling to part with the freedom that you were reminded of when it was dangled before your face once more.

As expected, when I saw Billie-Violet's little face, my freedom became a distant memory and our bond proved to be indestructible. Unfortunately for Bill, the second I saw my baby reach for my boob, a bizarre primal urge took over and I chucked her straight back on it. Bill's jaw dropped, all that hard work for nothing.

Sorry babe. Weaning fail.

I did manage to wean all of my children eventually. I promise that there isn't a seven-year-old having a cheeky suck while co-sleeping.

People will tell you when you should wean, they will tell you that a four-year-old suckling is gross, they will tell you that "if they're old enough to ask for it, they're too old". They will even throw bullshit studies at you to try to convince you that what they did is the right way to do it.

There is no right way, however having weaned two babies and had another two self-wean, I do know this:

1. The more formula you give them, the higher the chances are of them self-weaning, which can be a good thing and a bad thing.

2. When you start getting gross fingernail-scratching-on-blackboard sensations every time your baby/toddler suckles you, it could be time to wean.

I am a cold turkey kind of woman, probably because once I make up my mind about something I like it to be done, then and there. I cold turkey stopped smoking, I cold turkey stopped exercising and I cold turkey stopped breastfeeding.

When you stop breastfeeding your baby, the milk breaks down naturally. The idea is that if your baby stops sucking it out, your boobs stop piling it in. So the leftover milk inside your boobs just needs to break down slowly and your boobs will get the hint not to bother themselves with making more.

However, it hurts like a motherfucker when they fill up and like a seven-car pile-up it seems to take your boobs a long time to realise nobody at the front is getting through anymore. Meanwhile, you feel like you might blow up.

So the second time around, with Arlo, I had learnt a bit more about the patterns of my milk production. If I had a day off breastfeeding while at work, it took a few days of non-stop sucking to get the supply happening again. So when I was weaning, I went two days of refusing to feed Arlo and then I gave him a huge feed. It relieved my boobs so much to empty them again and having only done it once more, my boobs took the hint not to make anymore. It didn't throw Arlo too much either, the milk was already starting to taste weird after being in my boobs for two days so he wasn't hassling for more.

Problem solved, body mine again.

TOILET TRAINING

Some Queens think they've won when they manage to toilet train their kids early. They brag about it, compete over whose child trained earliest, like they will receive some sort of trophy. If there was a trophy, it would be the love heart shape of two golden bum cheeks bending over for you to wipe. Because the earlier you train, the longer you're wiping that shit for.

Billie-Violet was toilet trained young, she had to be, she was constantly getting urinary tract infections. When she had three urine tests come back positive, I took her for an ultrasound to make sure that everything was fine.

It was but the GP recommended that I toilet train her because little girls have a short urethra and pooing in her nappy, so close to her vagina, was giving her infections. Like it's that easy. "OK cool, I'll just go home and toilet train her before I put dinner on, cheers Doc."

I never thought that toilet training would be much of an issue in our house, we have so much nappy-free time that it's become the norm and nappy time is the abnormal. Yep, my house is like the hide and seek of poo. I often see a smear on a bum and have to go on a different type of Easter egg hunt. Admittedly it's annoying but it saves me so much cash on nappies.

The doc told me to stay home for two days, give her loads and loads of water, keep her nappy off and put the potty on the floor in the lounge room in front of the TV.

Obviously this plan needed altering, nearly two-year-olds don't care too much for TV, in fact sometimes I think the first three years are just a countdown until my kids will actually watch a whole TV show to give me a break. So I found myself chasing her around the house with the potty and eventually I caught a glorious wee in it.

Being an amateur I assumed this meant we were done, she was trained. The next day, after asking her four million times if she needed to go to the toilet, she shook her cute little head each time before she shat in the storage section at Ikea.

I was a cross between mortified and laughing hysterically. It was so funny. I didn't have any nappy wipes but parenthood has taught me that no matter where you are, a Queen is never far away. Between laughing and guarding the poo, trying to decide how to broach this, a Queen came over with a pile of nappy wipes and a doggy poo bag (side note: collect these for free at parks for nappies) and we both laughed as I cleaned it up and popped the treasure in my bag.

I like to think of toilet training as an outside job, no mess, no stress. Once Billie-Violet pooed in Bill's esky and when I asked her why, she replied that she didn't want the dog to eat it.

She was right, our dog delights in a fresh turd, which is kind of convenient, but your half-arsed bullshit attempts to stop the dog eating the shit is riddled with guilt. One of those situations where you try to stop him … but stop trying just before he gets there … and then you and dog can't look at one another properly, both feeling a deep sense of shame.

Toilet training is easiest when you don't have a time limit. Remember the golden bum trophy doesn't exist, so go slowly. The best piece of advice I ever received was: "If they don't get it in a week, it's too early. Pack it up and try again in a month."

Don't stress yourself out with smashing early milestones. When you wake up to your son standing over you, pissing on your hair like a scene out of The Power of One, it could be time to grab another packet of pull-ups.

Queens don't fail, they change their minds.

CHAPTER 4
The Rise of the Queens

When I first became a mum, I got an overwhelming urge to write.

I had been writing for years, emails, on Facebook, in my journal, but this was different. I wanted to share my shit, I needed to take myself seriously, I just needed to get it out.

With so much downtime as a mum, so much loneliness, I turned online hoping to connect with some other mums who might be feeling the same way. But every parenting forum I visited was so boring.

Was I destined to become boring now too? Were there any other options? What happened to all the funny chicks? Did mums morph into advertising's sanitised version of motherhood as the baby slid through the vaginal passage?

I was so confused, I couldn't find anything relatable on the internet, so I started up a blog. A real one, full of real stories, real questions, real ideas. It was well received when I shared it on Facebook. My friends hadn't had kids yet so they were intrigued by the posts about myself waking up early in the morning, too tired to get dressed, sitting on the couch breastfeeding, only to have shit explode out the sides of my daughter's nappy and nest itself into my pubes, while I sat there having an existential "who am I and why is there mustard-coloured shit in my fanny" moment.

I was surprised about how many people loved reading my stuff, I even remember the feeling the first time someone I knew "shared" one of my posts. It was crazy, to think that somebody liked reading something I wrote so much that they would attach themselves to it and sent it out into the wider world.

Over the years I haven't ever stopped. Writing lures me in with contrasting ideas and social stigmas that I feel the need to smash, never believing that I actually could but that opinion of mine wasn't going anywhere in a hurry. I had no options but to dress it up, hand it a cocktail, give it a huge middle finger and post it.

Never giving up on the dream of writing to a broader audience, I tried getting published a few times, sending my stuff to mothering websites. Most of the times I wouldn't hear back, sometimes I would get a thanks but no thanks. Over and over again, I heard the words "while you are very entertaining, it's not quite appropriate for our site at this time".

I don't remember feeling crushed by it or ever contemplating stopping, I didn't think of myself as a writer, I was a painter and a mother and a hairdresser and a whinging wife who wrote about every detail of life. Writing was something that I couldn't help but do, it was just me expressing myself. It's like if someone says that they hate the way you laugh, you don't change it because you can't. That's just the way you laugh and you certainly don't consider stopping, you just make a mental note that you are talking to an arsehole and move on with your life.

I started my "Constance Hall" Facebook page in 2015 when Bill moved out. He and I weren't getting on and so we decided that he should go for a while (sounds so civilised, I can assure you it wasn't).

My life was out of control, I had four kids, including six-month-old twins. On the rare occasion that I had enough time to stop and think about things, I'd realise how lonely I was.

One of the hardest parts of being on my own (besides the obvious that I had to do every fucking thing with no help and was run off my feet) was that I didn't have anyone to enjoy the kids with. Every cute thing that they did, every funny baby sound or adorable twin hug or hero Arlo moment was just for me. When you really enjoy something, your natural reaction is to share it, so not only were the tough times tough but the beautiful times were cut short too. I often found myself looking around to see if anyone else caught that moment, but of course nobody did.

I started my Facebook page, hoping to gather support and followers who could enjoy my moments with me. I have always had an opinion on everything — feminism, refugees, capital punishment — so I thought, why not share them in a public forum.

I was also sick to death of the witch-hunt on women. I felt as if the typical women's pages had been making a packet out of using women's curiosity or bitchiness as click bait and writing non-stop shit that tears women down and divides them. I found it painful to watch these sites throwing fuel on women and setting them alight all in order to get more clicks and make their money.

The page was about my life, my struggles, my opinions, the cute shit my kids were doing and whatever else popped into my head. People I didn't know started following and making really, really supportive comments.

The term "followers" never sat well with me, these women (and a few men) weren't following me or blindly doing what I told them to do or shadowing me — the way you envision when you hear the term followers. There isn't even a "follow" button on my Facebook, it was just a "like" button and I really liked them too.

Between October and December, I gained 1700 subscribers. I was stoked! That was so many rad legends who voluntarily wanted to read my shit. Mind-blowing stuff. People were tagging their friends in my stuff and their friends were liking it too. I would stalk the people who liked it and if anyone would share it, I would check on the reactions on their pages all day in disbelief that these strangers were talking about stuff that I had written.

I have a firm belief that in order to succeed in life, genuinely succeed with the kind of success that brings you long-term happiness, that you need to have the right intentions.

Intentions are the most important part of life. If your intentions are good, you will be backed by the universe, if they are bad you won't be.

That's not to say that ill-intended people or companies won't succeed, look at Donald Trump for example. He's made millions out of being a small-minded piglet, yet I would bet my life on his misery, no contentment can ever come from dividing and hurting people, he will have no peace and at some point he will come crashing down.

Unaware of the universe's plans for me, on New Year's Eve 2015, I wanted to post about my plans for the following year. I had been moved and shaken in the previous one by all of the trauma, all of the pain that I had read about in the media that I wanted to change. I wanted to be the change that I wanted to see in the world. I was tired of watching horrible events take place and then going back to deciding whether we should eat bolognese or schnitzels for dinner, unchanged. I was tired of the guilt that comes from being a comfortable Western woman while our brothers and sisters elsewhere suffer.

I wrote the following post:

I've heard a lot of people's attitudes are heading towards no more New Year's resolutions, with "you're fine as you are" quotes. I love that idea, I'm a huge advocate for loving yourself as you are, accepting yourself as the imperfect, dented, naive, wrinkly, fresh, unique masterpiece you have become.

But this year, I need to change.

When I was an apprentice hairdresser, I sponsored two kids. Most of my life I've donated what I could spare, the injustices of the world have always been so important to me.

However, when you live in middle-class Australia "what I could spare" has millions of different meanings:

- *change from a $400 dress?*
- *spare change after buying a $16 drink?*
- *$1 a day to offer a kid in Africa clean water and immunisations?*

What exactly can we spare?

Somewhere along the way, I started to have my own kids and used one excuse or another to pull back and close my eyes to what's really happening in the world, to what's happening beyond my clean and plentiful city.

In April, I watched an episode on 60 Minutes about the Kurdish women, left with no choice but to battle ISIS.

Watching a woman describe the moment she was running from the terror, holding her three-year-old boy in her arms when he was shot dead, right there in her arms.

Can you imagine anything more painful? My boy was three at the time, he still cruises the streets in my arms, the one place he knows he's safe.

That woman's story stuck with me.

Three months ago, sitting in my hammock, I was taking a moment out to scroll through Facebook and up popped a video of a little African child, no more than seven years old, starving to death, right there, so thirsty, malnourished and delirious that child's eyes had given up on this painful world, awaiting death for a final reprieve.

I watched on, forcing myself to stay focused and not become another rich white Australian annoyed that it was shared, angry because it bursts the little bubble we call home.

Next to me sat my chubby little Snow, stuffing her gob with a tray full of fresh fruit.

I don't need to explain why that little innocent African darling hasn't left me.

In September, a little boy's body washed up on a Turkish shore, trying to reach Canada fleeing war and terror, the sweet little boy drowned.

We all saw it, the images of Aylan Kurdi's lifeless little body lying in the cold water on the sand, fully dressed, with his little sneakers on.

I think about my little man putting on his sneakers in the morning, all excited for the day, full of hope and adventure.

Aylan would have been excited too, putting on his sneakers that morning, wondering what wonderful possibilities this new land might bring.

Something isn't letting me drop these images this year, something is making me want to change.

So a New Year's resolution is to change, I'm not going to donate "what I can spare". I'm actually going to go without something every week. And I've written this here to keep me in line, an insurance against my lazy side.

I never have to worry about food on my kids' tables, or even where my next mortgage repayment is coming from. How lucky am I?

It's time for me to give more, take less, keep my eyes open to this whole world and all of its inhabitants.

We are all one, all related, how can I enjoy this luscious life of healthy safe children and an abundance of resources if I'm turning my back on the needy.

If anybody knows of a great organisation that I can jump on board with,
I'd love to hear your suggestions.

Have a beautiful New Year, my friends.

Let's all try and remember it's never too late to make a difference.

Xxx

I had no idea when I posted this article that the universe was working its magic and creating me a path towards all my wildest dreams coming true. Why? Because it believed me to be ready …

My children had softened me, taught me to see the world through compassionate eyes. I had developed a message of love and wanted to help in some way, I wanted to push for change and my intentions were good.

The shittiest year of all shittiness was behind me and I had learnt, small things didn't bother me anymore, my weight problems were gone, I wasn't the clingy, needy loser that I thought I would always be. I had found my crown, I was a Queen and I believed in every woman's crown. My New Year's resolution was my final test and I had unknowingly passed it.

Not even a week later, I wrote a post about parent sex. I was driving from Margaret River, a glorious surfing town three hours south of Perth, to Denmark, an even more isolated town another four hours south.

We were in and out of reception, Bill was driving and I was thinking about the shag that we had had the day before, so I wrote about it and nervously read it to him.

We had "parent sex" yesterday.

You know what parent sex is, it's that 3.5 minutes you get in between changing nappies and making food,

Where you notice that all of your kids are pretty distracted.

Where you realise it's been almost a month since you banged and are starting to feel like flatmates,

Where your husband's seduction consists of one finger pointing towards the bedroom and the other hand on his dick,

Where you position the bed to have one foot against the door because for a loud bunch of kids, yours can be pretty quiet when they're sneaking up on people,

Where no matter how hot it is, you chuck the doona on top of yourselves in case someone manages to barge through and catch mummy and daddy doing "yoga" in bed,

It's a pretty romantic scene really, listening to Igglepiggle in the background, knowing your days are numbered when you hear the ad break.

Men are amazing and impressive creatures, by sheer determination, it's inspiring how one can manage to "finish" under such circumstances, us women aren't always so easy.

All the while gleefully thinking about how much of a sex goddess vixen you are and how your fella is finally going to stop being an arse for at least a whole day.

Well mine was pretty impressed, even if I just lay there, saggy boobs, baby belly pouch, hairy minge and all, he still thinks I'm amazing."

I was holding my breath, not knowing how Bill would react. He laughed and said "go on, post it".

So just like that, I did.

It was an hour until we were back with reception and my humble little post about the funny little three-minute shag had 12,000 likes. (That blog post reached 11.5 million people and was shared 20,000 times.)

Gobsmacked I was like, "what the actual fuck". Bill and I stared at each other for ages. The likes kept growing every single time I refreshed my screen. I couldn't focus on anything but my iPhone, when we finally got to the camping ground I was the shittiest mum there. Sitting on the curb with a bottle of cider, my iPhone and a little battery because god forbid I would run out of battery power, while my kids ran amok, skateboarding, creeping up to other families to score a sausage. I was in utter shock.

The next day was even more intense, news agencies around the world were writing stories about me. My sister, Stella, called me up crying, telling me how proud she was, my mum called, radio stations called, all wanting to know more about this three-minute shag, all wanting to know why the post went viral.

Now obviously it went viral for a few reasons — it was funny, it was relatable, so many couples out there were breathing a sigh of relief about their shitty sex lives not feeling that shitty after all and it was upbeat. Here I was not letting the pressures of a passionless bang get me down, I was proud of our three-minute romp, proud of my hairy bush. I felt sexy whether or not I was your typical "sexy" and people liked it. Queens felt validated, Queens felt like it was OK to be proud of their own hairy minges too.

If I have made just one Queen proud of her hairy minge, I have succeeded in life.

And it wasn't tearing men down. You don't need to bag blokes in order to bring up chicks, just like you don't need to stomp on another woman in order to raise yourself up. You can do that on your own.

By the following day, I had 70,000 Queens. I put my phone on the floor and flicked it away with my toe. The fear, the nerves … How could I write to all these people?

Finally, I went through and read the comments and I realised something — they are all my friends, just friends that I haven't ever met before. They are Queens, we are all Queens. So I wrote to them again and again and again and again. No nerves ever, as if we are all sharing a carton and bitching about the world, as if I had known them forever. I shared every bit of me with them and they did with me.

I never expected my writing to take off like it did, I thought like every other attempt at having a blog or website before, it would be just a hobby and I'd get lots of great feedback from people who knew and loved me and that would be that.

I hadn't ever really sat down and thought about how the past few years had changed me, but looking back, I have had some really life-changing years and it must show in my writing. It can't be a coincidence that straight after three years of hell — the sadness and depression and marriage breakdown — with normality slowly creeping back, I finally started to get traffic on a blog.

Maybe I had let go of my shit, or let go of an agenda or let go of trying to be someone else. Whatever it was, my posts were getting people from all over Australia messaging me, some telling me that they loved me, others wanting my advice. My advice? That was a first, even after having four kids, people never asked me for baby advice, probably because I'm in a constant fluster and there is nothing at all about me that resembles "shit together".

Since my Parent Sex post went viral, life has felt like somewhat of a dream, having just come out of the most depressing time of my life, reaching a point of wanting to give up, I am now faced with my every dream coming true. I am writing, whatever I want, whenever I want and publishing it myself.

That realisation comes with a tinge of sadness though. I think about Queens who have given up, Queens who couldn't see the light, who couldn't go on any further and I think that their dreams might have been around the corner too. I wish I could tell every single woman with depression or anxiety or who has gotten herself into a situation that she doesn't think she can get out of, that something life-changing could be around the corner. You just have to wait, it will come, this slump isn't forever.

As a writer, think of going viral as a wave, you wait your whole life for the wave to come and you have no idea when it will but when it does arrive, you have to be ready to ride it. And by ride it, I mean it needs to be backed up, otherwise you're left standing there with wet hair thinking, what the hell just happened? So I thank my lucky stars that I was prepared and I backed up that viral post with everything else that I've ever wanted to say if anyone was ever listening. And fuck me, it has paid off.

I have been asked countless times what my "secret" is. That question had me stumped for so long, I didn't know what my secret is. I'm not exactly a literacy genius. I sent a short story to a writing competition a few years ago and paid the extra seventy dollars to get it "reviewed" and they told me that the grammar and spelling was so poor, it barely made sense. Worst seventy bucks I have ever spent.

So what is my secret? I have dwelled on this question for months now and I have come to this conclusion: I love my audience, I wholeheartedly, emphatically love them. It wasn't until I became a Queen and fell deeply in love with my fellow Queens, that my posts started getting read, on a scale that I could never have imagined.

So I suppose instead of asking me what my secret is, people should ask themselves how much they love their audience. What message do you want to get across to them? If you had died and could get a message to your children, what would that be? Because that is a pure love, you wouldn't be bragging, you wouldn't be shaming, you would simply want them to know that they are doing really well, you would want to take away the guilt and pain, make them laugh, show them how truly magnificent they are, because they are.

I should know, since in my spare time I flick through pictures of the Queens who comment on my things, they all glow, they are all beautiful and I love them.

That's my secret. Love.

No matter how many times I get asked if being approached by Queens is annoying, I'm shocked by the question. While writing this on my laptop at a cafe, I was approached by four Queens — two with a pram, one with a baby in a carrier and one sans offspring.

Their words of encouragement and kindness left me speechless, I am not exaggerating when I say that I still have goosebumps. There is no bullshit between us, no small talk, they love me, they love each other and I love them. These particular Queens told me how lucky they feel to have met each other and it just reaffirmed my beliefs that we all need each other so much.

So to answer everyone's questions about what it's like to be recognised and approached, I feel like the luckiest person in the world. I never imagined that I would be let into women's lives like I am and I kick myself, every time a Queen introduces herself to me. I want to get her number, go hang out at her house, drink vodka with her … Seriously, I creep on to them more than they are expecting.

I feel this is just the beginning of a lifelong journey with Queens, our kids will be Queens or Queen lovers, we will break down barriers all over the world, celebrate each other and heal each other. Nothing's going to stop us.

The universe had given me this path and to honour it, I will never post anything dishonest, I will never post anything that didn't raise women up. I will use this platform to connect with those who need someone to share their days with and I will use this platform to help the Queens of this world who are in the most need, the most vulnerable Queens, the ones who believe that the world isn't listening. I will use this path that I am blessed with to show the world that the Queens are listening, because we are.

We want to make a difference. Queens have the best of intentions and that is why we are backed by the universe, that is why we succeed.

I still don't consider myself a writer, although I could never live without writing. But I am just a mum, who writes about her life, was given a path and won't tire of using that path to empower women and help the vulnerable.

CHAPTER 5
The Meaning of Love

I was supposed to marry a long-haired, strong-accented, tattooed gypsy man with a poetic licence to describe his love for me in three different languages.

We were supposed to get married in a registry office to circumvent our inevitably torn hearts since our passports belonged to different sides of the map.

And then we would have one baby, who would travel the world with us in our caravan learning the harmonica, learning how to paint, learning the languages of love and earth.

Only before I met this prince of romance …

I. Met. Bill.

A cockney-talking, shit-stirring carpenter who didn't have a current passport, frequents the pub, has no interest in music, art or languages, hates the beach, hates camping and loves FOOTBALL.

The most annoying of Bill's qualities: he is smug.

And I couldn't get the smug fucker out of my head.

Bill is the sharpest man I know, it doesn't matter how many times I try to get one over him, he catches me out.

He grew up in London, his dad was a painter-decorator and his mum looked after the kids. As the only boy with two sisters, he knows how to wind up the ladies. Many a glass of wine has been poured on my poor dear husband, usually by me but occasionally by another woman after she tires of his unique ability to piss people off.

He was that cheeky little kid in and out of trouble with the law, cruising the streets of London with his group of ratbag friends, the one who got away with everything due to some kind of charm or cockiness or possibly just because he doesn't seem to give a fuck if people don't like it.

That is what the smug prick does to me all day, every day. He pisses me off and then with his curly lip grin, he wins me over.

Funny always wins.

He moved to Australia seventeen years ago and turned over a new leaf. No more trouble, just hard work, a taste for Australian women and a fine-tuned appreciation for our pub culture.

Bill is obsessed with history, he loves nothing more than an expensive Scotch and a lent ear to offer up a history lecture. This is a rather redeeming quality of his, I feel like I can catch up on all of the stuff I missed at school by just tuning in for a few minutes. Followed by promptly tuning out because watching him gloat about his vast knowledge of World War II is both boring and annoying.

He loves soccer, would do anything for his mates and works hard — really, really hard. He owns and runs his own company which lays timber floors. Bill's on the tools all day then comes home to paperwork all night.

And for some reason, I fucking love him. He dances when he's happy, he's handsome, he climbs all over the kids amid tickle-monster attacks, he is generous and kind to everyone he meets and he was the first man I was ever with who didn't care if my pubes reached my knees or if my armpits stank. He doesn't even notice.

He looks after me and I don't care what anyone says — I am allowed to be a feminist who loves being looked after. I look after him too, like when he comes home from a night out, clinging to a kebab as if he just gave birth to it and it's his first-born son. I pry it out of his protective grip and help him eat it.

Bill and me are opposites. I spend my days at the beach gazing at the sun beaming off my little creations, spending too much money on unnecessary things such as $26 coconut yogurt and getting lost four times on my way to the supermarket, while Bill thrives on organisation, bills paid on time and sports ... lol.

Somehow it works, through all the ups and downs. Some days I just need to have a good cry and let Bill promise me that it's going to be OK. And it always is.

I have given up on us ever being an easy couple. Two extroverts who are so different, yet so similar, with huge fears of being controlled by someone else, who love each other so much but can become consumed by anger, probably won't ever get along.

Our counsellor described us as a non-complementary couple, explaining that this doesn't mean we are doomed, it means that we have to work harder than most couples. When he saw the disappointed look on my exhausted face, he added, "On the up side, other couples that I see usually come to me with a deep sense of boredom, a challenge you two will never face."

I took comfort in that, all couples have their own pile of shit to work through. The most important thing is that we decide to work through our shit instead of giving up. Maybe that's the definition of love, the belief that working through someone's pile of shit is more favourable than walking away from it.

My first real relationship at the age of sixteen was with an eighteen-year-old boy named John*, who was "too good" for me. He was brought up wealthy, private school educated, lived in a mansion, had sandy dark hair, unusually big lips and was fit and muscly. I thought he was hot, looking back he was not. But I hadn't exactly blossomed yet and my previous shag had bleached his hair bright orange and was "in between accommodation". So in comparison to that deranged hobo, John was hot.

I was living at my mum's house in Hilton, a suburb not far from Fremantle that had clusters of state housing. It was an attractive suburb for anyone interested in domestic violence or dealing meth. Or in our case, the affordability suited my mum and stepdad's bank balance for buying their first house. Hilton is a different story now — the house Bill and I bought is in a neighbouring suburb, because we can't afford to live in Hilton. It got cool.

I was shocked that John was interested in me, I wasn't from a particularly "desirable" family for someone from his world and I was going through my frizzy hair, thin eyebrows, overweight stage.

I was shy around his rich family. With good reason, as they put me down at every possible opportunity. When I say "they", I mean his mother, Ruth*, the "clairvoyant". There is no point arguing with a clairvoyant because they can just tell you that you are wrong. "The angels have told me that you are wrong." Hmmm, OK then, case closed.

John's dad had the cash and although he had separated from Ruth years before, watching her swan around town like Lady Muck was mind-blowing. I hadn't realised that gaining a hell of a lot of coin from a failed marriage was the type of achievement that made you better than everyone else but, I hadn't walked in her shoes … so maybe it did, who knows.

Ruth had been attractive her whole life and at fifty she still stood out as a good-looking woman, as was her daughter Amy*, a model. I was lucky enough to be shown photo after photo of John's sister every … single … day. And every conversation would somehow find its way back to the fact that "Amy's not attractive, she's stunning".

The pride that beamed out of Ruth when she spoke of Amy's international modelling career was enough to make even a fat little frizzy-haired thing like me feel sorry for Amy. What if she gets fat? What if she changes her mind?

How could anyone live with the pressure of Ruth's excitement?

Ruth enjoyed telling me stories about their past lives, like the time at dinner when she enlightened us with the story about how she, John and Amy were dolphins in past lives, swimming freely together. I loved dolphins, and excitedly told her that I hoped I was one too, trying to impress her by not spitting out my dinner and laughing hysterically at the bullshit she had just spun. But instead she shot me a dagger and said "no, YOU were never a Dolphin, just us". I slumped back in my chair, like a sea slug who needed to stop pretending to be a Dolphin.

I always knew that I had something to say, I just didn't know how to say it and I never felt it was worthy of being heard by a family of this demographic. So I kept to myself, despite disagreeing with the load of dribble that often came out of their mouths.

They were the most annoying type of rich, the ones who claimed that they were poor, while living in a mansion with a glorious swimming pool and no mortgage. You're not allowed to call yourself poor, that insults poor people.

I was a poor kid — well, compared to my friends and new boyfriend I was poor. Dump me in the middle of Africa and I'd be just as annoying as these arses calling myself poor but in comparison, I felt poor. Only they had already gobbled up the identity of "struggling" so I just stood there, hands in pockets, the sea slug with nothing to really offer anyone.

John realised a few times that he was "too good" for me and tried to dump me. I wasn't having a bar of it though, I picked up on his easily coerced personality, which probably was a result of his mother and her headstrong ways. He was so desperate to please his mother in any way possible that he almost cowered when I disagreed with him. He was so used to pleasing women and wasn't straying from that even with the one he was trying to rid himself of. Ironically, it was his mum who desperately wanted me out of his life and I was using her hard work to my advantage by keeping myself in it. Thanks Ruth.

Every time John dumped me, I insisted that we were still together and the poor bastard went along with it.

I was so scared of losing him, I thought he gave me an identity. I had felt so alone for so long, the teenage years had been rough on the old ego. John had a pack of friends, I only had two friends. That private school boys' club were the kind of guys who had rejected me throughout high school so even though these guys weren't particularly interesting, I was ecstatic to finally be in with them. To them I was somebody — I was John's girl. I had wanted to be someone's girl for so long, I had fantasised about wearing a guy's jumper to bed, having him buy me tampons, I even fantasised about having a fight with a boyfriend, just to feel part of something. It was safe being the girlfriend of a boy who was in the boys' club.

Despite knowing that I didn't belong, for the first time in my life I had something to clutch on to and I didn't want to let go. Shadowed by my lonely teenage years, I was so scared that without John I was nothing. My life without his warm house and family, the family that had been rejecting me for so long, would be empty.

Familiar with rejection, I became addicted to the feeling his family gave me, like it was my place in life and I could comfortably be the sea slug, as long as I was his sea slug.

It's an interesting approach, holding on to someone who's trying to run away. Your determination blocks out any pain that the rejection should be bringing and your heart becomes a battlefield. Every time I saw him, I was arming myself and fighting for my place in his life.

When I turned eighteen, John had been trying to break up with me for about six months, but I was still basically living at his house, sleeping with him and turning a blind eye to all the hints that he didn't want me around anymore.

Until one day, he turned to me in the car with a really odd expression on his face, his huge lips turned upside down like something out of a cartoon. He told me that he had slept with someone else.

This could be my earliest memory of the suffocating feeling of my heart being crushed. Everything went fuzzy and I felt like I was about to throw up. I made him pull over and I collapsed on some grass while he sat in the car considering how much better he felt now that he had gotten that off his chest.

I knew I had to get away from John now. I was making a fool of myself and even though I didn't have much pride at the time, I was still embarrassed. He had been talking to this other woman about me and how to get me out of his life. I was mortified. Like another woman had killed my mum or was laughing at the stains on my dirty undies, I felt so violated. I made him promise that he would never, ever see her again and I booked myself a one-way ticket to Melbourne.

Melbourne, where my dad lived, has been my refuge since I was little. Anything my dad lacked in financial support, he made up for in love and wisdom. My mum had just had her second baby to her new husband. When she was pregnant with their first baby, they began painting my bedroom light blue. I took the hint and moved into the garage. Now with the second one here, my mum's two-bedroom house had become one big nursery. At any time of the day when you walked in, you would get screamed at because the sound of your footsteps had woken up someone who had only just fallen asleep. I loved my mum but staying with her would only compound my depression.

The night before I left for Melbourne, John and I were invited to his mother's for dinner. I don't know why I accepted the invitation, I suppose on some level — no matter how little respect I had for them — I was still desperate to be accepted into their family.

When I got there, Ruth pulled me aside, she wanted to chat about John's indiscretion. I told her how heartbroken I was and she responded to me in a way that shouldn't have surprised me at all, yet it did.

"I knew you would be hurt and I knew that you would be taking to people about what John did so I did a bit of channeling and the angels have explained everything. You see, you and John were married in a past life, a very long time ago. He was very much in love with you but unfortunately you cheated on him with his best friend. So I guess that now he needed to do this and even up the score, even though it's not entirely even because John didn't sleep with your best friend, but you can understand now why he did it."

She didn't exactly say the words "So if you don't tell anyone what he did last week, I won't tell anyone what you did in a past life four million years ago WHICH NEVER ACTUALLY HAPPENED BECAUSE I AM A DELUSIONAL OLD COW". But we both knew that's what she meant.

I had to get out of there. I needed my dad.

In hindsight, I look back at my time with Ruth and realise she took me into her home, she loved her son, she was always kind to his friends, she believed in his future and she actually did teach me a lot about the universe and its powers. Was she really that horrible? Or did she just reflect my insecurities? Was I just so conditioned to carry my grudge on the privileged that I easily forgot all of the lovely things about her.

My dad at the time was sleeping on a couch at my nan's house. She had eleven kids, the majority of them had kids, and nobody ever made much cash so there were always plenty of people crashing back at nan's place in between accommodation. They are hilarious and loving and everything that a family should be. Everyone smokes a lot of pot, a few members have been in prison, some drink, some aren't even members of the family, we simply adopted them and they've been there ever since. I have more first cousins than I can count. What I love the most about this family is that no matter what they do to each other, they always get over it — life is too short for long-term grudges.

Dad said he didn't know where I would sleep but when he heard me burst into tears, he told me that we would figure it out. We did, with me sharing a bed with my cousin, on the other side of the wall to my dad's couch.

The chaos of Melbourne, the dysfunction of my marvellous family, and the excitement of being around my sister, Stella, healed me. I felt strong again, I felt confident. I had lost a lot of weight through stress, using my pain to motivate me to shed pounds that would make John regret ever mistreating me. I was fitting into Stella's clothes — she had always been too glamorous for Perth — so she handed me down a whole bunch of clothes and I felt like a million dollars.

I spent three months there and will never forget the perspective that distance offers. John and I were in contact, he told me that he wanted me to come home but wasn't sure if he wanted to be in a relationship with me anymore or not.

Instead of panic, those words just played on my mind. What did I want? Did I want to go back to the boy who would always be that bit "too good" for me? Did I really need that rejection in my life?

The moment that I realised that I didn't love John was the moment that I was explaining the situation to my dad, his humble pearls of wisdom had ways of shedding light and clarification on my soul.

We had walked down Separation Street, I was on my way out to meet my sister and her friends at a bar in Fitzroy, not far from my nan's house. Even though my dad had lost his driver's licence forever ago, he wanted to take me there so he walked me up the street and we caught a tram there together.

It wouldn't matter if we were cleaning shit out of toilets, my dad loved every second he got to spend with Stella and me.

I had been updating dad with the John scenario ever since I got there, he listened patiently and refrained from shaking me and screaming "WAKE UP, you are too good for this shit".

I filled him in on John's latest "I don't know if I want to be with you" comment. My golden dad replied: "So you know that you aren't making him happy anymore, yet you still want to be with him?"

Me: "Yep."

Dad: "Well baby, that is not love. Because I love you. All I want is for you to be happy, your happiness goes far beyond my wants. I loved your mother and I knew that she would be happier with someone else, so I had to leave. To truly love someone is to smile when they smile and to hurt when they hurt."

Me: "Dad, I think I'm too selfish for that kind of love. I don't care if I don't make him happy, I want him anyway."

Dad laughed and with his smiling blue eyes said to me: "You are lucky that I love you anyway, even if you are a selfish little turd, but that, my sweet girl, is not love."

And he was right, it wasn't love. A few months later after I had returned home and started a new job in a busy pub, I met a hot guy (hot by anyone's standards, not just compared to a deranged hobo) and I cheated on John. Just the once, I told him the next day. I knew that what I did was terrible and I knew that our relationship was over but most importantly, I knew that I had hurt him, yet I didn't feel any of the pain, hurting him didn't hurt me at all. It was just something I did.

John recovered, Ruth thanked her angels, and he is happily married now, to another Dolphin.

It would be more than ten years until I could finally grasp what my dad was talking about that night, when I finally hurt someone that I really did love. Bill. And once I realised what I had done, it hurt me like hell.

Over the years, I have realised that love is boring.

And a small part of me died.

Because I believed that love was explosions of life-threatening decisions, it inspired long-distance train rides with tear-soaked moleskine journals, it required heartache and a tingling golden warmth when rekindled. Love and passion were my guidelines, I followed my heart and it led me around and around in a cycle of confusion.

But love is not confusing.

Lust and desire are — they require chaos to fuel their journey. They throw you to the floor and tear out your heart to confirm that you're paying attention. Lust and desire die without attention, after injecting euphoria they sting you with mistrust and uncertainty.

Lust and desire have their place, they bring you back to your childhood and carry the blessing of the moment. People caught up in a lustful game are in the present, everything else fades away.

But love is bold, love needs no games.

Real love is unaccompanied, it needs no fireworks to justify its existence, nor must it travel with heartache or yearning. Love is bold enough to stand alone.

When you are ready, when you no longer need the game, the chase, the desire and the heartache to keep you focused, when you too are bold enough to stand alone, when you decide that you are enough, you are your own firework, you will be ready for love.

Because love is boring.

To anyone not ready to feel it, to anyone whose eyes are not open to it, to anyone who hasn't learnt it.

Love is contentment, companionship, love doesn't hurt.

I used to look at in-love couples and I thought they were so boring, I would run a mile from a situation like theirs. But these lovers, they weren't bored, they were calm, they had strength and soul. But I wasn't ready to see love yet.

I left Bill, on a mission to find my chaos, I left him because I was certain that love was heartache, love was all powerful and all-consuming, I didn't feel consumed anymore.

I wasn't ready for love.

When the chaos consumed me and I could no longer breathe, I went back to him. But I still wasn't ready for love.

Love is patient.

Love doesn't change to suit us, it waits for us to change and suit it.

The idea of being in a love that is boring is too confronting for someone who doesn't love themselves. Chaos distracts us from ever having to be still. Real love makes you look at yourself, there are no distractions, no drama to hide in.

But love is still. And so it waits.

For us to stop chasing, for us to stop needing rejection, for us to not need fuelling by a tidal wave of passion and pain, for us to learn to carry ourselves.

And when we finally learn, that we can live without yearning, that we can live without leaning on someone, that we are stable and strong and whole.

That we deserve to love, that a light can shine on us as brightly as can be and still have nothing to hide.

Love is there.

It is strong, meaningful, companionship, bold, warm and powerful. Love is calm.

Comparing real love to the fireworks and sparks of your past is an insult to love. Because love is the almighty conqueror that it knows no bounds.

Love is yours.

UNIVERSAL TRUTH

I talk about the universe a lot as if it's a person and not a thing. I do this because the universe is my power. The way some might worship a god, I bow down to the ocean, the stars, a tiny bird in a vast forest. Only I never really bow down, just a nod and a silent "we got this shit" every now and then.

I believe in karma, life lessons being gently nudged in your direction waiting for your response. Only, if like me, you are stubborn and hold on to your own ignorance, then things are hurled at you until, last resort, the universe will eventually pull that rock out from underneath you and watch you fall into a million pieces. Lesson learnt.

I have always wanted to be that intuitive chick, the sensitive one to all the universe's nudges and whispers. Instead I ignore them until I'm a crying mess on the floor, pregnant and alone with no options, nowhere to turn but around and around in circles until finally I turn to myself.

That's what happened when I was pregnant with the twins, everyone thought I had lost my mind. And I was on the verge of believing them.

My whole life felt like a chicken and an egg scenario with weight loss, weight gain and men.

I had waited years desperately trying to find that ultimate boyfriend, the one who would look after me, the one who would complete me and I had been determined that he was waiting for me on the other end of the scales. Fat me deserved nothing, skinny me deserved completion.

My dad had been dead for a year when I left Bill, I had spent twenty-eight years on this Earth knowing that through one man's eyes I was perfect and one year only seeing myself through Bill's eyes. As if blind I had never once bothered to look through my own.

I am an explorer of every emotion, I don my explorer helmet with a torch attached to it and I hunt around my brain, constantly asking the big questions: Am I happy? Is this marriage for me? Is he treating me the way I deserve to be treated? Am I living the life I was destined to live?

I just can't seem to do small talk with myself and unfortunately I have inflicted this curse on to the way I see Bill, always questioning his role in my life. Until one day my questions convinced my unsettled mind that I couldn't go on and he wasn't enough, that our life together wasn't for me.

I am glad I explored it, this would eventually be a tool in silencing the questions in my head. Yet I know that I trampled on the only heart I knew to be worthy of keeping safe, Bill's.

While curiosity didn't quite kill this cat, it dragged her tail-first around the block a few times, ensuring she was changed forever.

Pain is a warning that if we continue on this road, we will be changed. I suppose I needed change, we both did. So off I went, exploring my own mind and drawing conclusions that would change us forever.

Leaving Bill was one disaster after another.

I was too much, too intense, too aggressive. I had left a companionship wanting more fulfilment. Only nobody in their right mind wants to give you more fulfilment when you have only just met them.

I cringe now when I think about how I flaunted myself, trying to convince any potential lovers that I had my shit together when I was more than slightly broken.

I was thin, of course. I find my weight easier to control than my mind and I was convinced that being thin kept me worthy of that contentment that I believed I could see in every other couple.

Looking back, I can see the universe shaking its head at me, throwing me a couple of warnings so I would take the hint. No such luck, instead when I felt sad I numbed myself by drinking and texting boys.

I missed Bill, I missed my dad, I missed my home, but I didn't like the way that all this felt so I kept on going. Selfishly numbing myself.

So the universe realised I needed to be stopped and stopped I was. In the three months that I left my marriage, I spent less and less time with my children. Bill took them for three nights a week and

I also had them babysat often by my mother to facilitate my "lifestyle".

I fell pregnant to a guy who wouldn't piss on me if I was on fire and had to have an abortion that he didn't pay for. I couldn't even bring myself to tell my friends who didn't seem to be too interested in the downward spiral of my life anymore. Every time the kids went to Bill's, I'd find myself drunk and alone. Turns out being thin didn't get me a boyfriend or more fulfilment.

So I turned back to Bill and begrudgingly, he took me back.

But the universe was on a roll now, why would it stop? I hadn't really learnt anything, jumping straight back to the safety of Bill. I was yet to turn into the only person who could make any lasting differences … Me.

So the punches kept rolling and even though Bill and I had hardly had sex and he withdrew when we did, I became pregnant with the twins.

Being pregnant to a man who hates you is kind of like being locked in a prison cell with the owner of the bank that you just tried to rob. There is a constant switch between wanting to kill each other, screaming matches and a deadly silence — for nine whole months.

I am not the silent-treatment type but Bill is. In fact, he plays a lot of the typically "feminine" roles during a fight — he angry cleans. When we are arguing, he makes a huge deal about cleaning the house. I used to cringe and try to take over because I know that angry cleaning is just somebody's way of pointing out that you aren't cleaning. But over the years I have learnt to sit back and enjoy the fact that my house is getting cleaned, sometimes I take photos of him, create a little collage so I can send it to him just to piss him off further. That never goes down too well.

Being pregnant with twins, I was cornered, even more needy than ever, but Bill didn't want a bar of it. I suspected he was enjoying the silent treatment while I was going out of my mind. Hyperventilating every day, every single thought about my horrific future. All I ever wanted was love, to be loved completely by a man and now I was stuck with the only one I wanted, the only one I could possibly forge a relationship with and he hated me ... and to top everything off, I was fat.

And there was nothing I could do about it. I couldn't do what I had done my whole life and make myself feel worthy with the instant gratification of a man's attention nor could I lose weight. Control had been taken out of my hands. I would never meet another man because I was destined to be a fat single mum of four kids. Rock bottom.

My life was over. I hated myself, I hated Bill for punishing me. On my mission to be skinny and loved, I had found myself alone and fat.

Well played universe.

BECOMING COMPLETE

Gratefulness is not an emotion that happens to you instantly, gratefulness comes as a reflection. This was not my time for gratefulness.

Because when the universe throws shit at you, hurling steaming piles of cow shit in your face, nobody in their right mind would say "fuck, thanks for that, mate".

You don't say thanks when a guy you're engaged to pops up on your hairdresser's Tinder.

You don't say thanks while waiting in the line at an abortion clinic.

You don't say thanks when you find blood in your poo and are being wheeled into theatre waiting for a hot doctor to put a camera up your haemorrhoid-riddled arse.

You don't say thanks the first time the child you live for tells you with certainty that she hates you.

You don't say thanks when you get fired.

And you never say thanks when you send your best friend a text message that says "I just wish I was dead".

But there will come a day when the pain is replaced with insight and with that insight come a big fat fucking thank you.

The universe is a force with invested interests in your wellbeing.

It's driven entirely by us Queens being the best that we can be. The universe is motivated by finding a Queen her crown and it will stop at nothing until it appears firmly on our heads.

I thought I was a Queen, I had no idea that I was trapped, trapped by a belief system that my world would be complete if Bill could love me more and Bill would love me more if I was skinny. But there was no crown in sight.

When everything is pulled away from you and all your options are snatched from your reach, you are forced to feel it, your usual ability to numb yourself with distractions disappears, and you are left with no choice but to feel, confront, live.

A repetitive theme in my life: fucking shit up happens quickly, rebuilding is slow.

I never woke up after a night of crying consistently for six hours with a vision of a shiny crown. Crowns are slowly built on your head and you don't even know it's happening.

All of the shit that I had done to myself — every bit of loneliness and fatness — was there to change my beliefs system and gradually I had to find myself as a Queen whose value was not a reflection of how a man saw me. My co-dependence had no choice but to become independence. I was forced to value myself as a good friend, a mother who would die for her children, an artist, a hilarious Queen who didn't need her dad, who didn't need Bill, whose life was worth so much more than a number on the scales.

A year of being that woman and I was changed — for good. After the twins came out of my tummy, I was completely shocked by my behaviour.

I wasn't on my usual weight-loss regime, I wasn't pushing them around in a pram up hills and walking for hours on end, cutting out carbs or trying some new flash diet. Everyone I knew was waiting for me to lose the weight, they kept reminding me "You'll lose the weight, you always have done before and being a single mum of four, you're going to want to at least be skinny".

But I didn't. That drive for skinny, that drive to be filled up by a man, that drive to be completed had, just like many a lover in my past, disappeared.

My pining for completion was gone — I was complete.

The universe does this for you, your knocks and your blows are an offering of self-worth. Your greatest times of despair are your greatest assets, you need to hold on and let that loving universe break you down in order to alter your every single shitty, co-dependent, self-doubting, body-shaming, needy trait. Let the universe complete you.

Now I walk through my house like the Rad-Bitch legend that I am, maybe Bill's not talking to me, I have more curves than a race track, my dad's still dead and I love myself. That rock that was pulled out from underneath me so many times? It has become me as firm as the crown that sits on my head.

Yes, I still cry all the time and totally lose my shit and have a messy house and haven't washed my hair in three weeks, but I'm a Queen, no self-loathing here.

Now that universe of ours … has ulterior motives.

There is a reason that Queenhood is so high on the universe's agenda. Self-empowered women are the change this world is in dying need of. There is no stopping the power of a woman who believes in herself. Whether it is the reaching out of a hand to the less advantaged or just a crown tip to a Queen whose three-year-old just got done for shoplifting.

Queens don't leave anybody behind. We use all that compassion and all that empathy and we run wild with it.

Through hardship the universe changes Queens.

It may steal your social life, test your marriage, radically change your body and take no prisoners when conquering your hygiene.

However, amongst all of this change, the real essence of your transformation comes in the softening.

Learning to let go of a perfect house, learning to not let small marital wars take their toll and learning to appreciate a social system inclusive of your new baby or new divorce.

All on your journey to softening into a compassionate mother.

Softening to life
Softening to love
Softening into yourself

Motherhood softens us in ways that the little tough nut hard-shelled super bitch never dreamt possible.

Queenhood is the universe's most well-planned move. It grabs women and feeds them a whole bunch of fucked-up disasters, one of which comes in the form of motherhood that consequently injects them with an overdose of compassion. This compassion forces Queens to stop ignoring the injustices of our world and to start acting, making moves to secure a safer future for all of its inhabitants and the planet itself.

Our job is to channel that compassion but beware because it can easily become a weakness and can be used against us.

Don't let all of the universe's hard work in fine-tuning a system that gives it to you exactly when you need it be wasted.

The world needs change, it needs a hero. Queens are today's heroes, it's time to start acting like them because we hold the power, we are raising tomorrow's heroes, we are privy to the world's suffering and we don't ignore that shit.

We are blessed to be the majority, the low-income earners, the ones in flawed marriages, the owners of the bodies that contradict society's image of perfect. That makes us the majority and unlike the minority we can change the world with little to no effort.

Queens, stop and pick up that woman and her baby catching a bus in the rain, pick your favourite charity and go without something each week to help them, show your children how fucking fantastic you fundamentally believe you look in that bikini. Tell a friend who has recently had her first baby how much you hated life during those first four months, reassure her it gets better, give her your phone number.

Show your children what kindness looks like so they too can be kind.

Show the world what kindness looks like because the world has gone without for too long.

CHAPTER 6
Relationships Can Get Fucked

I hate to break it to you Queens but that funny cute boyfriend you picked up one night at a party and have been inseparable from ever since? The one you decided to spend the rest of your life with because he's cool, has rad tats and loves the fuck out of your every move? That guy who takes on the world with you. Yeah, that guy.

He'll probably be a selfish arsehole for a year or so, you'll probably spend that year with your jaw so far dropped that it's caressing your sore tits.

I can't help you, this is a biological fact. But I can warn you and hopefully eradicate some of the shock. Sometimes we can approach our own lives with more patience and less panic when we know that we are not alone.

Some people think that these warnings make me a man hater, rather it's quite the opposite. I love men, so much so that I have decided to warn Queens that the majority of them turn into selfish tosspots when babies come out. I do this in the hope of saving marriages. If Queenies know that most men are behaving like this, even that hot guy you see at the park playing football with his young son, then you may be more inclined to work things out with your tosspot instead of leaving him, foolishly believing the grass will be greener somewhere else. It won't. And you're welcome, men.

Babies change women automatically — their safety, health, feeding and sleeping routines stress the absolute shit out of us. It's like a panic attack, and we lash out at anyone who questions us. Men stress too, but it's more the "sit back on the couch, crack open a beer and text their mum to ask her to come over and help him 'babysit' next week when you go out for the first time" kind of stress.

Firstly, can we all stop calling it babysitting when they are your own kids? I didn't babysit them while you went to work on Monday, so you're not babysitting them when I go out, get shit-faced and bitch about you all Saturday night.

Men do change eventually — they just take their sweet time. They don't like to put too much pressure on themselves with family commitments, bless.

I'm sure there's a biological reason that harks back to the caveman era as to why men struggle with the newborn stage and then seem to thrive when their children get older. I went to university to study psychology because this sort of thing fascinated me, unfortunately I dropped out after two weeks so I can't be of any assistance with the real scientific facts, you will just have to take my word for it.

The following is a list of the annoying things blokes do when you have a baby:

- Pretend to sleep through the baby crying or actually sleep though. I don't know which is worse.

- Snore. I know it's not their fault and they were doing it before the baby came but fuck me dead, it's so annoying. Especially if you're sleeping lightly which is the only kind of sleeping new mums can do. It's just so in and out and in and out. I will admit, at 4am I have prayed for it to stop and considered the breathing part collateral damage if it was to magically stop too.

- Not trust your instincts and call their mums or sisters to second-guess the things you are doing.

- Expect you to ask their permission to go to the shops without the baby. "I'm going to the supermarket, honey" to which they respond with "Oh… are you just going to leave the baby here?"

- Ask "what have you done all day?" With four kids, I don't need to be justifying myself to anybody. After my first though, I often caught myself explaining, "I've been so busy, the baby cried all day, I haven't had a chance to even sit down". Now, I'm not responding other than with a "fuck off".

- Hand you the baby when it has shat. We have a rule, if you smelt, saw or in anyway discovered the shitty nappy, it's your responsibility to clean it. Even worse is when they pretend they didn't see it. Gives me the rage!!

- Inform you of anything that insinuates you are somehow more of a parent than them. "The baby's awake" or "I think the baby's hungry". How many times have I preached the words "WE ARE BOTH PARENTS". Don't inform me, fix it.

I'm not going to lie and say that my relationship was amazing before I had kids, Bill and I have always had a really fucked element, for so many reasons. Thank fuck, I love the guy so much.

We started off on the wrong foot since I had been shagging one of his hipster mates. That was a doomed arrangement that fizzled because no matter how incredible I am, I only have one vagina. This guy needed a selection of vaginas that I could not offer. So I fucked him off/he fucked me off, the details don't matter… and travelled around Europe for a few months.

When I arrived home, I considered myself quite the worldly, exotic, cultured Queen. I was saying "hola" instead of "hi" and "gracias" instead of "thanks". Part of me wants to cringe but the other part of me still thinks of myself as exotic and cultured — I'm torn.

Bill was the hipster's unhipster mate, so when I met him I wasn't impressed, intrigued but not impressed. Bill, on the other hand, was extremely impressed, he had heard so many bad things about me and my psycho ways that when he realised I was capable of a normal conversation, even if it was in somewhat broken Spanish, he was impressed.

I met him at a pub in Fremantle, I was of course pulling off drunk chic, Bill was with the hipster I used to bang. Out of the corner of my eye, I saw said hipster try to hide behind a wooden beam. If there's anything that pisses me off, it's guys you used to shag hiding from you in public.

Yes, I admit, there are some guys that I used to shag who I now hide from but only the stalker loser types … Hmmmm maybe to that hipster I am the stalker loser type. Interesting.

So I went outside for a cigarette (don't worry Queens, I've since dropkicked that habit) and obviously intrigued by my psycho drunk chicness, Bill followed me and introduced himself, hoping to be able to return to his mates with a funny story about something mental that dribbled out of my mouth. Bill was not expecting to be completely blown away by my Rad Bitch, hilarious queenly ways.

A week later, he came into the barber shop where I worked to have his hair cut. I didn't do it, someone else did, but I knew he was listening in to every word of conversation I was having with my client.

Two weeks later, I was at the beach, gliding across the grassy area. As I floated past a group of people, sitting down enjoying a beer, Bill looked up at me and said: "I'm seeing you everywhere."

To which I responded: "It's fate, baby."

And it was. Nine years later, I'm still floating past him at every opportunity, only now he's not watching me and instead of cheeky, suggestive statements, I'm telling him to get fucked and he's giving me the finger.

We had so many common interests, like beer and pubs and drinking booze in the morning after a big night. In this day and age, it's really hard to find someone who you not only have these things in common with but who also keeps you in stitches of laughter all the time. So needless to say we began our morally challenged relationship.

Bill and I suffered our ups and downs for a year, we had hilarious moments and tragic ones. I think, in general, you would class ours as a fairly unhealthy relationship, we would fight in public and break up most weeks. It was never going to be an easy road. Two extremely extroverted people, constantly fighting over who's the funniest, both drinking too much booze.

Everyone wanted us to break up for good. We responded by announcing my pregnancy.

Boom. Try telling Queenie what to do again, I dare you!

I'm not advocating unhealthy relationships, I'm advocating against judging my unhealthy relationship. There's a difference.

Pregnancy is the beginning of your "new" relationship, only you don't know you're having a new relationship yet. It's very confusing.

Marriage counselling has taught me a lot of things, including the fact that inside every relationship is various new relationships. Your relationship needs reinventing as your circumstances change.

The first huge change was the imminent arrival of our first baby. All of a sudden we went from equals who could live our lives freely without really needing to consult one another to me being annoyed all the time at Bill's choices and only being able to see how they affected me.

If he got drunk, I would hate him, if he was out too late, I would resent him. Now we were a real partnership and needed to run every fucking thing past each other in order to avoid a fight.

Now that we have four kids, I like to look back on that time and laugh to myself, like what the fuck was wrong with us, we couldn't even workshop the easiest and simplest situation. There really were fuck-all pressures compared to life today. But it was all new to us and I really believe, even now, that there is no harder time than when I brought home my first baby.

So if you have brought home a baby, please don't ever let anyone say to you: "You have nothing to worry about, try having two or five." Whatever. There is nothing harder than your first, you have every right to be off complaining to your friends and rocking in the corner. It is a big fucking deal, Queenie.

I used to watch American rom-coms and wonder where that guy is, the one who dotes on his pregnant girlfriend like the fertility goddess she is. I would watch the preggo montages of hubs rubbing the belly and they would both laugh like the smug, loved-up arseholes that they were. My boyfriend was in the other room on his computer, or watching the football, or out with friends while I was in my room watching Grey's Anatomy on a portable DVD player resting on my belly. Every now and then the baby would kick and the DVD player and I would laugh, smugly with pride at our growing baby and I would hope she looked like me and not too much like the DVD player.

This would mark the beginning of my journey with FML. Over the next year, I would say "Fuck My Life" in my head five-hundred times a day.

Welcome to your new relationship that is basically one big "whose life is worse" competition! And guess what Queenie, there are no winners.

When you have a newborn, you don't "wake up" anymore — it's more about waiting for an acceptable hour to move from your sleep-wake position in your bedroom to the lounge room. So when you do make that move and you enviously spy your husband actually waking up, it's only natural for your first sentence to be a big fat complaint.

"I didn't get any sleep last night, like sweet fuck-all."

This would be greeted with a cup of tea from your fella, right? Or an arms-around-the-shoulders supportive "what can I do to help?" type statement, right?

Wrong.

In the whose-life-is-worse competition, all complaints are met with another complaint.

"Yeah well, you're not the only one who's tired around here, try going to work after a night of no sleep."

At first you're shocked — can I not even complain about my life without him thinking it's a dig? It wasn't even a dig, we were talking about me!! But of course never to be one to rise above it, you can't help but respond with another competitive statement like …

"Fuck off!! I heard you snoring all night, you don't know the meaning of the word tired. The baby was up every thirty minutes. I literally Have. Not. Slept."

And off he goes to work. That went well.

So why do we stay? If we hate each other so much?

Because most of the time (not always, some men are actual real-life dicks) the hate isn't real and all you both need is a goddamn motherfucking break to remind each other how much you love each other.

Having children can give you superficial hatred for your lover, you can't believe how annoying, lazy and unfair each other is. But deep down you are bonded, along with the baby comes an invisible super glue that keeps you there for those flashing moments of extreme happiness. For me, there is no greater happiness than the happiness I've felt when my little toddler screams her head off accompanied by some weird Bollywood-style happy dance when Bill pulls up after work.

This is love, this is our new love.

Somewhere amongst all of our arguments, lack of sleep and financial pressures, in between the birth of our first and second baby, we found the time to get hitched. So that's gotta stand for something. Yes, we broke up the night before the wedding and called the whole thing off. I made it down that aisle, nothing was gonna stop me from rocking that spraytan and dress, I didn't care if I was met by nobody at the altar, I couldn't care less if I had to drag a friend's boyfriend out of the crowd to be the stand-in. I was getting married.

But Bill was waiting. With tears pouring down his face at my sheer Queenliness.

After the birth of our second baby, things started going downhill again… big surprise. It was like we didn't expect anything of one another anymore. I stopped complaining about his lack of presence in our marriage. He worked all the time — I would sit on the couch and text friends while watching Game of Thrones, Bill would do "paperwork" on his computer which, regardless of whether or not that was true, it felt like a big fat "fuck off, I don't want to hang out with you, loser".

And I am not a loser.

I realised that I had been begging the man, dying for his attention, bribing the man to join us, to be a part of us. I was craving a family and I thoroughly believed that Bill just wasn't getting it. He wasn't a team player, his work was about him, his social life was about him and to be honest I was just so done with wanting to be wanted.

I couldn't chase this family dream anymore.

I remember a few poignant moments about the demise of us. I remember Bill working on his computer late one night, I had been in my room putting Arlo to sleep, overthinking everything. I went out to his office (which was just a corner in our laundry, next to our fridge that for some reason has never been able to fit in our kitchen).

"Bill," I said to the back of his head as he scrolled the news on his computer.

He said nothing.

"Bill, I'm really unhappy."

He still said nothing.

A deep sense of relief washed over me, like I suddenly realised that my misery was valid. This guy doesn't give a fuck about me, I can let go now, no more trying, accept the things I cannot change.

That weekend, Bill went out with my lifelong enemies, his friends.
Only I didn't see them as enemies anymore, I had let go of Bill, they could have him.

I went to bed with the kids, Arlo tossed and turned, I woke up to breastfeed him, looked at my phone and saw that it was 2am, no missed call from Bill, no messages and it was the strangest feeling. As far back as I could remember, all I had was anxiety about Bill's whereabouts, always calling him, even chucking the kids in the car to go and drag him out of the places he was. I was so scared of losing him, so scared he would cheat on me, scared he wouldn't come home. But this night I felt relieved, I didn't want to see him, couldn't be bothered dealing with him and for the first time since I met him, I hoped that he wouldn't come home.

I am a loyal person, the only times that I have cheated on anyone was on my way out of a relationship. I have never cheated and tried to get away with it. I haven't been in many serious relationships before Bill but the ones I have been in, I'm usually the committed type.

Leaving someone for someone else or ending a relationship and landing in someone else's arms is a great way of distracting yourself from the pain of a break-up … if you're sixteen. When you are twenty-eight with two kids and a mortgage, it's a really, really bad idea.

I began reforming my relationships with the men I knew. I don't want to say that I was desperate for attention because that feels like I am somehow shifting some of the blame on to Bill, whereas the blame is entirely my fault. My immaturity or my ego or my lack of strength are solely to blame.

If I could turn back the clock, I would have done things so much differently. Would I still have left him? Hell yes. He was being a selfish prick at the time and he desperately needed a kick up the arse. But what I gave him was not a kick up the arse, I kicked him to the curb and broke him, the man that I loved.

You see Bill and I had broken up so many times, sometimes I moved back into my mum's house, sometimes I took off to Melbourne and once I moved into a share house with my friend's big brother. Yet every single time I went back to him and ended up in a similar place to where I started. Why? Because I absolutely loved the man.

So this time I was determined. I moved out, so terrified to face the world without him yet so desperate for some male attention I possibly did the worst thing I could do in my situation. I told Bill that there was a huge possibility that he and I would rekindle after this "break" yet I formed other relationships and began sleeping with other men.

It didn't take Bill long to find out. I can safely say I crushed my husband's heart. It was like he blinked and I moved myself and our children out of the house, leaving it a cold and empty shell for him to drown in.

I was so confused, the unit I lived in was only around the corner from our family home and I would force myself to not show up at what was now his house and curl up into bed with him. I was yearning for a life, a life away from my children, I wanted to be present with a man, I wanted to be desired by a man, I wanted to feel like me again. I missed my own identity and felt so trapped by my entire family.

All of a sudden Bill was taking the children a few nights a week and I had a life again, albeit a life I could barely enjoy after the path of destruction I had left behind. But it was still a life, something I felt I had lost since motherhood and wifehood took over.

Bill would visit me all of the time, I could see a deep sadness in his eyes for the loss of me, his wifey, his family, a sadness that I had exempted myself from with a selfish distraction. I was torn and it was tearing him apart.

After about four months, a car crash, too many drunken nights out and meaningless relationships, I looked at myself in the mirror and instead of seeing that identity that I had been searching for, I saw nothing. In the year I had lost my dad, I also lost my marriage, made a fool of myself, tried to raise children on my own and I didn't know where to turn. I was lost.

And the only person who has ever been able to find me when I am lost is Bill. By then Bill had met someone else too. It didn't crush me at all, I knew I deserved that and I knew he deserved that. But nothing was going to stop me from capitalising on the one thing that I can always rely to have on my side. Fate, baby.

Bill didn't take too much convincing. When someone cheats on you and dumps you even though part of you hates them, another part of you craves them with more intensity than you have ever felt before. Because you are in agony and they caused it, so surely they can fix it.

Fixing it is another story but, yes, I got my Bill back. He let me and the kids move straight back in and told me that he loved me but there was resentment, so much resentment.

I thought that Bill and I had a bad relationship before I left him. I was wrong, as what we were now experiencing was relationship hell, held together by our children and a fear of the misery that we had only just overcome.

I was happy to be with him but I have always been happy to be with him. It's his lack of desire for me that drives me away and now he had no desire for me at all. I could feel it when he hugged me, taste it when he kissed me, hear it when he spoke to me. Our relationship felt empty.

Bill and I made an effort to have sex, two lovers trying to show love with an expression of love, that involved no love. It defined disconnection. Every other day we discussed breaking up, neither of us wanted to put the children through another move, so we had decided that this time he would go.

Within three months of us reuniting, we had had sex three times and on each time Bill had withdrawn. The withdrawal method had worked fine for us in the past so I was surprised when I started feeling a familiar urge to curl up on the couch and have a nap in the middle of the day.

I took a pregnancy test. It could not have been worse news when the two little blue lines popped up. Bill was at the shops with his mate and I sent him a photo of the positive pregnancy test. When he and his friend walked through the door, Bill mouthed the words "Are you pregnant?" to me.

"Yep," I replied and the look of horror on Bill's face was priceless. "FUCK."

It's cool, I was thinking the same thing. I was mainly annoyed that I had to feel like shit until I could get an appointment for an abortion. There was no way I was keeping this baby, since Bill and I barely spoke to one another.

I had left a miserable relationship to find my freedom, I didn't like my freedom so I returned to an even more miserable relationship and this little embryo inside my belly simply represented more misery and less freedom.

Amongst all of this misery, Bill and I had flashes, snippets, lightning bolts of happiness — moments where we would remember how much we love each other and for however brief the moment, all the resentment would wash away, giving us both clarity of why we love each other.

In these moments we would joke that maybe the baby was fate, maybe the baby will show us how to be together again? Despite knowing our last baby only divided us further, we tried to fool ourselves. Love wants to prevail, love will let you lie to yourself, love will trick you. So we made about eight appointments for abortions and then either cancelled or didn't show up. Thankfully, the Queens who work at abortion clinics are employed solely on their queenly abilities to handle other Queens with compassion and love. So they never told me that I had to pay a cancellation fee or banned me from the clinic.

One day we set aside an hour, went to the place by the beach where we got married, and sat down with the intention that we would make our decision. We agree an abortion was the best option, the appointment was for the morning … Come the morning we didn't go.

Amongst all of this confusion, I was feeling like utter crap. I made an appointment to see my obstetrician Doctor Heart as I wanted to know if the pregnancy was ectopic or not viable for some reason. For all I knew, we could have been stressing out over a decision that wasn't in our hands at all.

His clinic staff were so happy to see me, glad I was breeding again. I didn't break it to them that I wasn't sure if I was keeping it or not. It's not in my nature to keep things to myself but I wasn't feeling like myself at the time so I just kept my gob shut.

Doctor Heart is such a gentleman, his big hands helped me on to his bed, he turned on his ultrasound machine, rubbed the cold jelly on my belly and then his face dropped.

"What?" I was scared. What the fuck was it? Something with two heads?

"Twins," he responded.

I don't think I have ever been more shocked in my life, we don't have twins in the family.

So there goes my abortion. Some women struggle with the decision to have an abortion. I can honestly say that I have never regretted one, the choice to not have a baby to a random bloke whose name I can't remember will always be above anything, my right.

But this was different, this was a friendship, a bond, besties, siblings, closer than siblings, twins! A party in my belly, for all I know one is holding the other's hair back while she spews from drinking too much amniotic fluid the night before. It was a miracle, a blessing. I couldn't abort twins.

I texted the picture to Bill and placed him on suicide watch for the next forty weeks.

The next year was horrendous, full of fighting, crying, screaming. I was being punished for my adultery, for being a shit wife. I knew I was a shit wife but I was so tired of the punishment, I felt like he only got back with me to punish me, I felt like he got me pregnant on purpose to punish me, I felt like my only options were to be punished forever or to be a single mum with four kids aged five and under. I was at my most miserable and I required a lot of help, help that I couldn't get from the one person who had always helped me, the one person who usually pulled me out of the shit, Bill. I knew he wanted to help but he just couldn't move past his resentment.

Slowly we got better. After someone has been unfaithful, it's a two steps forward and one step back kind of process. Like any normal couple, we would fight over daily shit. With twin babies, it's kind of impossible to get along, there is no sleep to be had, everyone's in a bad mood. Bill was working all day, while I was expected to have dinner on and present a reasonably tidy house. I was definitely not reaching those targets.

Me: "Bill, can you do the school run? I actually want to kill myself when I have to get the twins out of the car and into their prams and Arlo just loses his shit begging to play at the park, it's just a fucking nightmare."

Bill: "No, I have to go to WORK, you know that thing that keeps this house afloat?"

Me: "Actually it's me who keeps this house afloat by keeping all the kids alive but if you can't help me with the kids then I don't see the point in you even coming home. Just go out with all your mates after work."

Bill: "OK cool, so you can go and fuck someone else while I'm out, sounds like a good plan."

Me: "I knew you'd say that, you always have to go there, don't bother coming home at all, move in with a friend, I don't need this shit in my life, go fuck yourself."

Bill: "Good, done, enjoy your life."

Bill would move out for about a month at a time, I would get used to being on my own, he would miss us and come home, and I would be relieved because I missed him. But in no time at all, something small and insignificant would happen again and we would go through the whole cycle again.

I was constantly telling the kids that "Dad's working away again" and being kids they believed me. They missed him terribly but they got on with it.

The rest of us could learn a thing or two about resilience from children.

It was gradually happening less and less, as Bill and I were both coming to the realisation that fighting was only tearing us apart and we actually wanted to be together so subconsciously we began to ignore each other's little digs.

If there is one thing I have learnt about fighting from being in love with a man who I technically don't get on with very well is that you can't avoid the little digs and snaps, they are part of a healthy marriage. People get angry, they get in bad moods and they say snarky little comments throughout the day.

It's up to the other person who is (hopefully) not in a shit mood to ignore the snaps and digs, then instead of a full-blown argument, you end up just having one little shit comment that you can bring up later if it feels unjust.

So instead of focusing on never venting or releasing something that's bothering you, try to work on your reactions when your partner does. I know I should have stayed at uni and become a marriage counsellor — you know what they say "Those who can't, teach".

Everything was plodding along fine until the twins were six months old. Bill had a huge job on with a commercial property so he was only able to work at night. Because it was school holidays, it would be tough for him to sleep during the day, so I decided to take the kids away to our friend's holiday house and give him a break.

It wasn't easy, having the four kids away and no husband there to help me. The twins were still at that age where they wanted to be held 24/7 and the bigger kids just wanted to run wild all day, every day. Holidays with kids are unpaid hard labour, yet I continue to go on them every chance I get. I feel as though I can forgive myself for all my parental fails if I can at least create these types of memories for them.

On the third day of the trip, I received a text message that made my stomach throw up my brekkie. One of my bestest friends, Freya, and her husband had been to a funeral the day before. They are more like family to us, we stay with them a lot and vice versa, so naturally after the funeral they would stay at our place, after meeting Bill for a drink at a pub.

That's where Bill met her, a much older woman who had been at the same funeral. Bill had called me around 9pm and said he was about to go home. I told him to call me when he did. He never called.

In the morning I spoke to Bill, he still seemed a bit drunk, was kind of rude and was on his way to work.

And then I got the message — a three-way message between Freya, Bill and myself. My heart still skips a beat when I think about it now.

"Bill, I think you need to tell Constance what I saw you doing last night."

As it turns out Bill did go home, they all went back to our house and had a few drinks. Freya told the other woman that Bill was married to her close friend and that we had four kids together. The woman seemed surprised but not enough to deter her from what she was about to do. Later on, Freya woke up to go to the toilet and heard noises coming from my bedroom. She walked in on Bill and this lady shagging in my bed.

In the end it was Freya who told me, Bill didn't want to admit it and Freya couldn't handle the thought of me not knowing.

My heart was crushed. Despite it being only 9am, I started sculling wine. Freya was on her way to me, bringing Valium, and to look after my children for the following four days.

The emotional rollercoaster you go on after someone cheats on you is possibly the most irrational place I have ever been. I was crying, feeling both furious and devastated. I was pining for him, wanting my kids close, then wanting them gone. I was drunk for two days then determined to stay sober. The most surprising things that I remember feeling after the initial haze cleared were:

1. Regret. For everything I had done to Bill. You see when someone cheats on you, you have an overwhelming urge to bring them as close to you as you possibly can. Despite the betrayal, you believe that only they can heal you and fix your wounds. They were your rock and they crumbled underneath you without any warning. After returning home, I did just that, I pulled him in as close as I could (before kicking him out and then making him come to me again), convincing myself that everything we had wasn't gone. Bill was happy to do anything he could to help me and save us. That gave me so much regret, I was getting an intensive short course on exactly how agonising it is to know that your partner is in the arms of another, has another's smell on them, had taken pleasure in another's body. I now knew exactly how deeply I had hurt Bill. Only when I hurt him, I hadn't given him the chance to be healed by drawing me in. I had walked away, not looked back, leaving Bill to suffer on his own and now I knew exactly how deeply he had suffered.

2. Relief. I felt like I had been punished for so long over the things that I had done to Bill, that I didn't have an even playing field in my own marriage. Every argument was won by him bringing up my indiscretions and while half the time I didn't have any more "sorries" left in me, I felt sorry and thus he won the argument. I guess now I felt like I could stand up a bit straighter, I could leave that shitty decision behind me. It had been weighing me down for so long and now for some weird reason I felt as if my pain was paying for my mistakes, through suffering I was earning back my rights in my marriage.

It didn't take me too long to stop hurting, like I said I am resilient. I have been resilient my whole life, my psychologist told me that I was, by nature, one of the most resilient women she had met.

I have learnt in my life that dwelling on painful memories wouldn't help anything so I am a master of distraction.

Jasmine, my wise and glorious psychologist, also gave me another piece of solid advice that I always pass on to anybody facing a situation where their partner has hurt them.

She told me to not make any decisions straight away. Let him stay in the house if you want him there, ask him to leave if you need to be away from him. But you need help with the kids right now, there is no point in making your life any harder than it needs to be. Do some painting, or spend a lot of time with friends, focus on you, build your strength back up with walks, chats, creativity, whatever you need to do to feel good about yourself on a daily basis. Set a date, somewhere down the track, maybe in three months, maybe in six months but on that date make your decision about your marriage. Not right now when you are too hurt and life is just too hard for you to deal with the added burden of making a life-changing decision. Relieve yourself of that decision for the time being.

I felt so relieved hearing those words. I was putting so much pressure on myself to either forgive him or kick him out, everyone was asking me

"what are you going to do?" and "you haven't forgiven him, have you?"
All I wanted to do was distract myself for a little while (it certainly did not
help that I had broadcasted what had happened to my Facebook friends
while I was on my two-day bender after receiving that text message.
By the time I awoke from my slumber, it had one hundred and fifty
comments on it.) I became the Queen of the sentence "my psychologist
says I don't have to make that decision at the moment" and that shut
everyone up.

Before Bill and I went through any of this, I didn't have strong
thoughts on cheating, I had neither a here nor there opinion on
the matter. When friends discussed desires to embark on some
extramarital activity, I was more of a "well, you only live once" kind
of girl. I was the one with a cheeky grin telling my friends: "Think
about your death bed, you're not going to be lying there grateful that
you were a 'good wife', you're going to be reminiscing about all of
your adventures."

While I felt a lot of empathy for those who had been through relationship
indiscretions, I didn't have the experience that I think is needed to really
be there for someone in need. Now if anybody, a guy or a girl, comes up to
me talking about an affair or a fling or shares the brilliant epiphany that
they are planning to run away with someone, I am incredibly forceful with
my warnings.

I grab them by the collar, put my face within a millimetre of theirs, and
assertively tell them: "Don't do it. If your fella is being a twat and you don't
feel like you love him anymore then go. Go and he could change, go and
he will realise what he has lost, or just go. But remember this, if you start
sleeping with someone else, he will find out, you will crush him and no
matter how convincingly your anger is telling you that you want to crush

him, it is lying, you do not. Have a wank or spend all your money on a new outfit, go out and get drunk or buy yourself a week's holiday in a resort. Cheating will ruin you guys for such an incredibly long time, I wouldn't wish it on my worst enemy. If you cheat on him and he finds out, every single thing that you have ever complained about him doing or not doing will become invalid. I left Bill because I wanted change, I wanted him to be present in our marriage, I realised that I didn't want to be without him and when I came back to him, I had fucked him over so badly that the presence I had wanted was so much further out of reach than I could have ever imagined. If he doesn't find out (which he will) you will have to live with the guilt for the rest of your life and that guilt will ruin your bond with each other. Cheating is never a good idea, the grass is never greener."

By then I have usually scared most of my friends so far off the idea of cheating and hanging out with me that I am no longer burdened with their relationship issues.

Knowing when to walk away is just as important as knowing when to stay. Only Queenie knows when she has reached her limits. All I am trying to say is don't do what I did, don't do something you can't take back because anger has convinced you that you will never want to take it back, most of the time you do. Today I can't imagine my life without Bill — he is the most annoying, sometimes self-centred, often neglectful of my womanly needs man I have ever known. He is also my family, my best friend, he has our smell, he is the funniest, the most hard-working companion and lover I have ever known. I often think we were tested to our limits and we passed, other times I think we are the only person as fucked up as the other, and through a stroke of luck we found each other.

WHEN IS IT TIME FOR MARRIAGE COUNSELLING?
Obviously that's different for everyone, for me however it's ALWAYS.

I don't think you can get counselling too soon. I'd have a PP if I could, like a personal assistant but a personal psychologist who follows you around debriefing your day for you.

Most men, on the other hand, hate the idea of counselling. Why do men always say no to counselling until it's too late? They wait until their relationship is dangling by a thread, looking up at them with scissors in one hand and giving the finger with the other. You are not going there for your past, you are going there to protect your future.

Bill and I like to sit down in therapy and blurt out all the shit the other one has done in the history of our entire relationship.

Me: "Well Bill went and fucked ..... behind my back."
Bill: "I wouldn't have fucked ..... if you hadn't have been fucking ....."
Me: "We were on a motherfucking break!!!"
Bill: "It's not a fucking break if you're the only one who knows you're on a break."

And so on and so on.

Then we usually start to laugh as we are both well aware of how bogan we come across.

I have caught our counsellor looking at his watch and then out the window, I think I even saw a thought bubble pop up over his head that said: "If I wanted to spend my life watching Jerry Springer, I wouldn't have bothered studying for six years. I wonder what the surf's like today? Breeze is in ... fuck these two are still going!"

As much as nutting out some of the past is a healthy and productive step, you also need to remember that counselling should feel safe, like a place that you go to and put structures in place, rules to your arguing. Agreements on things that you both don't want to happen in the future anymore. Relationship therapy should be about love, even the decision to go there shows that you both still believe in each other.

I will never forget the day that our marriage counsellor made this very significant statement: "When a couple has children, it's common for a natural divide to take place and if it's not stopped, it will only grow bigger. You both begin to look elsewhere for your needs, needs that used to be fulfilled by each other. Men tend to go to their friends for fun, they stop seeing their wives as fun, and ladies tend to go to their friends for intimacy, to have deep conversations and feel supported."

That rung true for me, we were both doing it. I saw Bill's friends as my mortal enemies because they were constantly dragging him away from us, while I would really look forward to him leaving in the mornings so I could call my friends and have real conversations, about how I'm really feeling because I sure as shit wasn't saying any of it to Bill.

Losing that connection, losing that friendship, was huge for me. I always said to Bill that I felt lonely. I told him, my doctors and my psychologist, anyone who would listen, that I found parenthood and wifehood lonely. I thought I'd gotten married to avoid loneliness, only now it was bringing me the total opposite.

I won't be a miserable bitch and say that marriage is like a prison sentence but … OK I am and it is. You're less approachable to new friends because you're married so people assume you have all the company you need, you don't go out much because it's always a drama that starts a fight or requires a babysitter. Or maybe you just realised that the only real reason you went out all the time when you were younger was less about your passion for beer and more about your drive to pick up. You spend waaaaaaay too much time at home, thinking about all the things you hate about your life, such as your husband, but is probably really more about your general lack of a nanny and a cleaner and a personal psychologist to talk you into getting out of the car when you've parked at the supermarket. Somehow we just like to funnel our problems into blaming the one we love instead of wondering if it really is everything else.

So we began to work on things step by step. Relationships are like buildings, they can fall over quickly after a disaster but rebuilding them will always be a step-by-step process, there are no shortcuts.

RELATIONSHIPS AND MONEY

Learning to not live off your OWN money can be particularly hard for Queens, that should come as no surprise.

I never had much cash, I went from being a hairdressing apprentice to a travelling bum, to a qualified hairdresser on $22 an hour to an expectant mum who was living off my BF. Bill was a carpenter, he had his own business and Perth was in the midst of a mining boom when we met so being a tradesman was losing the working-class stigma and turning into quite a successful career. So needless to say, I was pretty confident that the change I found in Bill's dirty washing would put me in a better financial position than I was in before so I wasn't too concerned about cashola.

I should have been though, no matter how poor I was on my measly hairdressing wage, there was one thing my money was and Bill's just wasn't — mine. I learnt very quickly that working for it is easier than asking for it, asking anyone for money sucks. Even if you are heavily pregnant with no maternity leave, even if you have four children, no self-respecting Queen should ever have to ask for money.

Some Queens go straight back to work earning their own money, others decide to stay at home for ever and ever — none deserve to beg their boyfriend or justify what they need the money for or wait for their weekly payment.

If you do decide to be a stay-at-home Queen, you need to be assertive, put shit in place to make sure you don't end up feeling powerless and stuck.

When I had my first baby, Bill was giving me money when I asked for it, which made me feel like I needed to justify what I needed it for. While I fully appreciate a budget and a team effort to reach financial goals, no one in a relationship should ever feel as though they are having their spending examined with a fine-tooth comb while the other holds the power. Only equal relationship are successful ones.

So I became a dodgy little fucker, some ways that I would save money were:

- **Cashies.** I would give haircuts and not tell Bill, at one point I had $670 cash hidden in a sock.

- **Medicare.** I would pay all of my medical bills with Bill's money and have the rebate deposited into my private bank account.

- **Outright robbery.** Bill is a light sleeper who always knows how much money he has on him so my burgling sprees were limited to the nights he would go out with friends, get drunk and come home. When he passed out, I would rob him. He would check his wallet in the morning to see how much cash he blew and feel guilty that he spent so much, so he wouldn't question me at all.

I don't feel bad about the above behaviour, if you don't give your partner full access to the finances, you're creating a barrier between you, it's asking for trouble. I have never been one to sit back and let life's injustices drown me. Fuck off, I'm a get-even kind of gal.

Once I cut a magnificent Queen's hair, she had been married three times, was a sucker for love and a lover of men who suck. Who can't relate to this Queen?

She shared with me her interesting history. First marriage, young and dumb, both poor but in love, he had a drinking problem, she was supporting them both emotionally and financially and ended up cutting him loose.

Second husband was rich, she had a baby to him, he would deposit her "allowance" in her bank account every week and if she spent it too soon, he would deposit more. He was careful to never let her in on their finances, old-fashioned maybe, or maybe just a wank stain who didn't think it was her right to see his money. (She had only quit her job to raise a baby that would carry on your legacy, give you grandkids and love you until your stingy old bum sagged around your ankles.) She told me that for some reason she burnt though their money like there was no tomorrow.

Final husband, similar financial position as her previous husband. Despite not having any children with my Queen, he was an open book, insisted they have joint bank accounts and always encouraged her to have an active role in budgeting, with free rein to spend as she pleased.

"And you know what?" Queen told me. "I hardly spend a cent of it, I feel responsible for it, I have goals for it, I certainly don't want to waste our money."

So the moral to Queen Bee's story is not to find a guy who will let you download the app to his internet banking but rather, even if you are a stay-at-home mum and you don't pay the bills, demand it!! It's so much better for your own wellbeing knowing that you are a part of your own financial situation and not just some beggar with a tin saying "please sir, can I have some more" every time moneybags walks past.

The number of arguments Bill and I have over money is ridiculous, mainly due to the fact that I would buy a $99 peanut if the wrapper said "irresistible peanut" and Bill is moneywise to really annoying extents.

He came home from work once on a hot day, I was there, windows open, air-con on, in my undies on the couch, drinking a cider, expecting my happy husband to tell me that I was an irresistible peanut, yet instead he goes: "Con, look, there's a fiver just flew out the window, grab it!" Confused and a bit drunk, the poor traveller inside me was worried about losing a five-dollar note and I jumped up to go and find it.

Bill continues: "Quick, there's a tenner too, just flying out the door, look."

"What the fuck are you on about?" I snapped.

"Well, sitting here with all the doors and windows open while the air-conditioner's on is like throwing money out the window, seriously you might as well just empty your wallet at the door."

That kind of shit really annoys me, I flicked the bird at his smug face and took my irresistible self to bed.

It's a really hard concept to grasp and I totally get that it's a tough transition for blokes too. One minute you're earning your own cash, no fucks needed for anyone who isn't yourself, and the next you got your bird knocked up and she's getting a massage, new hairstyle and pedicure for herself and her dog all at the same time and gleefully calling out to the receptionist "just put it all on my card". Only her card is your card, she's only three weeks pregnant and has already spent your life savings of $25,000 on preparing her new maternity-themed wardrobe.

For fucks sakes, would you give a Queen a break!! She's creating goddamn life, what have you done today?

I don't think the idea of "our" money truly kicks in for a long time, some men never get it, so much so they are what we usually refer to as exes. Other men take to it so naturally, wanting nothing more than for their glorious wives to feel comfortable with what she is entitled to, we refer to them as keepers. The majority of us have men who are somewhere in the middle. Learning to share is a joint effort, together you will get there.

Whether you are a woman or a man, having a career as a parent is a privilege. You are privileged to not have to sacrifice your career in order to parent, you are privileged to have someone prepared to do that for you. It does not make you smarter, more successful, more valuable or in more control of the income than the partner who stays at home and paves a safe and healthy environment for the kids.

There is a shitload of stress around cash, it's a shitty subject to get your head around, this new dynamic of sharing one income, all the while you're not sleeping and a little gremlin has turned your life upside down. Always remember that it isn't unusual to argue over money, show me a couple who doesn't and I will show you the bottle of Prozac in their bathroom cupboards. What I'm encouraging Queens to do is make sure that those arguments are on an even playing field. One where you feel entitled to the money you are spending, regardless of whether you are the one earning it, because trust me, even if you are not earning it, you are earning it.

Bill and I have been together on and off for nine years. We fought about money today and I'm sure that in five years time we will fight about money again. It's an argument that never goes away.

At the end of the day, money isn't real, it can buy you new tits, temporary happiness and really expensive pinot noir but it isn't real. Your babies are real, health is real, love is real but money is just a piece of paper that divides demographics, cultures and families. Nobody says on their death bed that they wish they earned more money.

FUCKING

Some Queens get so goddamn horny when they're pregnant that they're googling threesome porn all day and fingering themselves in the toilets at their obstetrician appointment. Others couldn't think of anything worse, you already have a whole human up there, you don't need another end of another one. The visuals of a baby's head getting nudged by a wang bobbing up and down is just fifty shades of wrong.

Like Queens, all men are different. Some find themselves holding an erection with a sad look on their faces every time wifey waddles past ignoring said wang. While others think it's kind of weird and would rather shag the inside of their elbow than go near that maternal lump of complaining female.

Sex when you're heavily pregnant makes you feel kind of like that cow in the anti-dairy campaigns, the one getting fisted by a farmer who just stands there with an unimpressed look on her face.

Only you're lying on your side trying to hide the fact that you're on your iPhone checking your Facebook notifications, thinking, yay an old friend from high school that you haven't seen in fifteen years has uploaded a photo of a fancy-looking boiled egg that she has made for dinner. Sounds boring but it's fuckloads more riveting than the farmer having his way with your rear end. You wouldn't usually comment but fuck it, you're bored, give the egg some love. And it's over, you'll both live to see another day.

The only time most chicks put themselves through it is when they are desperately trying to get the baby out. I don't even know if there's any truth to the theory that semen can bring on labour, I don't know anybody who has ever had any luck with it. I'm tempted to believe that the whole thing has been orchestrated by some hornbag doctor and scientists who are tired of standing around with their erections in their hands while their pregnant Queens waddle straight past them, waiting at the hospital to high-five all the baby daddies who bring their wives in for their final checkups. Well played hornbags … Well played.

I hope you had fun boys, coz you ain't getting nothing once this baby's out. People tend to bring over all sorts of presents when a baby is born, flowers, clothes, champagne and chocolate, all of which are totally amazing and appreciated. However, why nobody is bringing over a massive pile of porn is beyond me. Now there is a business idea, porn delivery packs for new dads. I could be a millionaire if I applied myself.

There are so many reasons why we don't want to bang once we have babies, to list a few:

- **Breastfeeding.** There is definitely some kind of biological, hormonal, pheromoney type thing happening, I could be sure if I went to uni for more than two weeks. Your body is so not interested in cock, it's scared of cock, it only wants to feed your baby, your body thinks that you and the cock you rode in on can fuck right off. Cock means more babies, your body just wants to care for this one, so body rejects cock, baby is your numero uno now. If you don't listen to the little voice inside your head that is your hormones trying to convince you that cock is an evil devil-worshipping enemy, then the hormones trap you with a dry fanny, there is nothing less smooth operator than wedging a wang into a dry fanny. Wang be gone.

- **You're buggered.** The only thing I'm getting jiggy with at bedtime is my pillow, you fantasise about bed all day and then get two hours to yourself before the baby wakes you up for a drink. If an excited spouse tries to creep into bed with you and encroach on a percentage of that two hours to yourself, they would more likely get executed than ridden.

- **You are touched out.** The baby is in your arms constantly, the toddlers are pulling your hair and throwing shit at you all day, even the dog is draining the life out of you. You really need some space. In fact an invisible electric fence that gives every human who enters your personal space an electric shock would suffice, a cock shock for all cocks within a metre radius.

Don't be alarmed hubsters, your penis will come back on our agenda. When we want more children. No, I'm kidding! We will crave the cock again. Most wifeys really do want some intimacy again when things with our new baby settle down.

Queens, make sure your husbands know not to take this personally, rejection feels horrible whether it's at a job interview or in your bathroom holding your own erection. Erection-rejection is serious and needs to be talked about with sensitivity. If our men know that it's not just them, they may find it easier to swallow.

I would like to take this opportunity to speak some love, you see I am a "really can't be fucked fucking" kind of Queen. I'm tired, busy and I'm just not that horny these days. However, when I have decided it was time to fuck Bill — and trust me we don't need that much time — I have felt so goddamn happy.

The stress of our everyday lives turn us into flatmates, resentment takes over and we forget who we are. Sex brings us closer, at the moment we are only really doing it about once a week and while it may only last 3.5 minutes, the closeness lasts all week. I think if Bill and I could find more time to bang, we might find ourselves fighting a shitload less. Go on girls, give him one.

THE OPPOSITE SEX

Marrying a Queen does not come with a rule book and for this, I sympathise with men. Some of them didn't even know they were marrying one but before long, regardless of who we are, Queenhood gets to all women and a lot of relationships (and men) need reprogramming.

- Go easy on him, he is in as much shock over his uselessness with a new baby as you are.

- Find out which ones of your friends you can bitch about him to, without them disliking him afterwards. I always gravitate to my friends who respond to my angry husband texts with something like "OMG he's such an arse, should move into a commune with my BF and they can be selfish and lazy and stroke each other's erections for eternity. Hey, do you guys wanna come over for a BBQ on the weekend?"

- I hate the term date night, but have a date night, time away from the baby will breathe new life into you as a couple.

- Have boundaries, even in your arguments. Don't be afraid to argue but have cut-off points, if either of you say anything really below the belt, like name calling, put up your boundary, pull the pin and refuse to continue talking. Nobody deserves to be belittled, abused, threatened or made to feel worthless.

- Keep an eye on the bigger picture, which is impossible when you've had no sleep. I feel like an arsehole for suggesting it, but try anyway to take deep breaths, be grateful for what you do have, health food, Nutella, porn, whatever.

- If you can't get on and every time you cross paths you're arguing, put a thirty-minute problem-solving time in place for discussing the things that have pissed you off this week. This gives you both time to calm down after the annoying act, so that when your weekly session comes around, you can discuss it with more clarity. It's not clouded with anger that could make you say horrendous things, things that will tear away small bits of your foundation.

- Don't settle for shit. Sometimes we think we are doing the right thing by just expecting something shit. We are not doing our husbands any favours by accepting or ignoring their shitty behaviour, because when you fall out of love with them and dump them for the twenty-something pool cleaner, they will feel ripped off. It's so important to ask for what you need, tell them where you think they are falling short, give them a chance to fix it before it's too late. Trust me, there is always a time where it's too late, even if you think you are being "understanding", nobody wants to be walked all over forever.

- Learn the difference between typical behaviour and abusive behaviour. Forgiveness and an easy-going nature is vital in a healthy relationship yet incredibly dangerous in an abusive one. If you don't know the difference and sometimes the lines can seem blurred, talk to friends, talk to your doctor, talk to a psychologist. Our country is in the midst of a domestic violence epidemic. Emotional abuse, financial control and physical threats or violence are never acceptable.

Educate your bloke about what it feels like to be a mother. Because I believe it feels very different to being childless and to being a father. For example, the sound of a baby crying can be just another sound to a man. I am so often shocked by my male mates when their baby is crying and they carry on chatting or working or doing whatever they are doing. As a woman you feel that sound, you don't just hear it. When our new baby cries, we physically hurt, all other sounds are blocked out and nothing else comes close in importance. It's so hard to drive when your baby is screaming, I have pulled over in the most dangerous places just to make sure my baby was OK because I physically could not carry on until I settled her.

When I can't see one of my kids, I lose a bit of control. Bill is rational, he retraces steps and finds our kid, I start doing laps in my backyard screaming my head off. I don't think anyone can really understand why we go a little crazy after having babies, they are so deeply attached to our bodies, emotions, souls. The umbilical cord may have been physically severed but never really goes anywhere.

From personal experience, the male's role in parenthood becomes priceless, the woman's is right from the beginning.

Women without blokes stand up and kick goals in their stead but I appreciate what Bill does so much for our children now. At first I was concerned, I felt like I was always going to be doing this on my own. If I knew then what I know now I would have relaxed. There wasn't much room for him in my little newborn love affair. There is so much room for him now, while my place as a mum was instantaneous, his place as a dad grew and is still growing.

I realise that not all relationships are destined to succeed after children, sometimes the strength isn't there, the foundations aren't there. Queenie needs some goddamn space or the guy is a bit of a knob-jockey, it happens. I know, shock horror, some Queens accidentally breed with fuckwits. Some fuckwits only reveal themselves after the baby pops out, like "TA-DAAAAAH I'm actually a fuckwit!!!"

Of course it's possible that some Queens are fuckwits too, but I am not in the business of treating Queens like anything but Queens so that is all that I have to say on that matter.

Most of the time, even if your boyfriend acts like tits on a bull when your baby arrives, he will get there. I hope. Nearly all of my friends called me after their babies were born (I'm that friend you can bitch about your husbands to until the cows come home). They were wanting divorce papers but within no time, the marriage was straight back to love, laughing, fucking and YouTubing cat videos together.

When I first had my babies, I was convinced that Bill was the worst dad in the world. He didn't do night feeds or get up in the mornings, he wasn't spending any time with us, he worked all the time and thought that that made him the most godly man on the planet.

Fast forward to now and I'm not going to say that he is the best dad in the world, but a lot of days he puts me to shame. He plays with the kids more than I do, does dinner, changes the twins' nappies. When I hear them waking up in the middle of the night, I'm inclined to leave them to sort themselves out while Bill's straight up to check on them.

Parenthood was an instant change for me and a gradual one for Bill, but I think in the end we have both been equally changed. That's why I often tell my friends to hang in there, bitch and complain until the cows (husbands) come home but hang in there, because there is nothing worse than breaking up with a guy only to find out that all that hard work you put into them has paid off and they are now "the perfect guy" … only for another Queen.

GET A LIFE

Around the same time that I realised Bill and I weren't ever going to be the perfect couple, I figured out that all of the "perfect couples" I knew were secretly either considering counselling or downloading Tinder.

I never realised how healing the truth can be. People pretending to be perfect parents or in perfect marriages are really damaging for the rest of us wondering why our lives are spiralling out of control. The truth about everyone else's lives yanks a massive weight off our shoulders, gives us permission to have no idea what the fuck is going on. Lets us breathe.

Counselling taught us a lot about how unimportant our arguments were. Our counsellor once warned us: "Don't lose the relationship winning the argument." Bill and I are so opinionated and passionate and so much emphasis was placed on being right. But no amount of rights would ever mean as much to us as each other.

We still fight — Bill still gives me the silent treatment and I still threaten to leave him but the three things that stop us from being tragic bogans throwing each other's stuff out on to the road are:

- Knowing that this is normal — calmness and pleasantries are wonderful but rare.

- Knowing that end game, I want him. I spent a lot of our relationship with doubts, I don't doubt now.

- The kids. My aunty, who works in child protection, has told me about the long-term effects on children whose parents are constantly fighting. That alone is enough to keep my mouth shut. No matter how furious I am, I prefer to get in my car, drive around the corner and from my high horse, text him a three-page novel rather than fight in front of the kids. I'd prefer to be wrong, swallow my pride and let Bill gloat than inflict my kids with avoidable anxiety.

There is another massive change, one thing that I owe my marriage to, one thing if there was ever a "secret" to my happiness, I cannot ignore.

I. Got. A. Life.

Because I don't do "stay-at-home mum" very well. I don't do "wife life" well. Some people smash it, I do not. I need something else, that's just the way I roll. So staying at home, waiting for Bill to come home, having dinner ready and folding washing made me hate him, hate my life and hate myself.

Anyone telling me that I can't go to work because it doesn't make economic sense for our family is pretty much digging my grave. I need to exhibit art or do a few hairdressing shifts or study or write. I need to value myself in a way that isn't just a pat on the back for finding the most direct route for a sweet potato into a toddler's tummy. That's not enough for me, it's not OK for people to expect me to lose myself in that role.

When I'm at home five days a week while Bill works, I obsess on the things he says to me, the four walls cave in and all I think about are our arguments or the lack of fulfillment that this household is bringing me. By the time he gets home, I'm guns blazing.

The number of times people told me that I had to stay at home because Bill earned more money than me and my wage wouldn't cover daycare fees is unbelievable. I didn't care that my hairdresser's wage wouldn't cover daycare, I didn't care that I painted seventeen pieces for an exhibition and sold only two and I didn't care that there is "no money in blogging" — I deserved my life, you only live it once. So I insisted that our combined income pays for daycare, not every day but I need two days a week to myself. Yes, I want to be with my children but I need a life too.

And almost like magic when I got that life, my relationship healed. The resentment washed away because we both have ambitions, we both have goals and we are both raising these precious children.

Finally then could I love Bill properly and all Bill's ever really wanted was to be loved properly, so we began to heal. So much washed away once I started to prioritise my life, my happiness. There is nothing selfish about putting yourself first. Insist on having a life, it can be the greatest gift you can give your family.

I used to have a terrible habit of panicking when we fought, no matter how many times we argued, I would convince myself we were over.

One day someone told me this wise mantra: "Something ended badly hasn't ended at all." I love that, it calms me down. It's just a fight, life goes on, Con and Bill go on.

The sign for me that a relationship is working is not a magic overnight fix, as magic overnight fixes leave us all disappointed with the following night's unfix. It's simply less resentment, fewer fights, more laughter than before.

At the end of the day, Bill has changed, we both have even though neither of us really noticed we had.

Bill is everything to us, the kids adore him and my love for him is deeper than I ever expected to love anyone. I am so proud that we've made it, that no matter how many opportunities we were given to walk, we chose to stay. We have both put up with, forgiven and accepted more shit from each other than most people could imagine … and it's strengthened us.

I love him. Did I mention that? I really do love you Bill, if you ever bother to read this. You are the absolute shit.

CHAPTER 7
The Art of Raising Children

I used to believe that Queens were in the midst of a war and we needed to band together, arm up and defend ourselves pronto.

I believed that parental guilt was the Queens' enemy number one and it was my mission to wipe the fucker out. Until I had an epiphany: if parental guilt is so bad, why is it a natural occurrence, why are we all getting slammed with it, what does parental guilt want from us?

It occurred to me that the one thing Queens fear the most is being a shit mum because obviously we want the absolute best for our darling babies and nothing is scarier than thinking we are doing them an injustice by not being enough for them. Queens are always enough.

But shit mums don't get parental guilt, it never occurs to an abusive or neglectful mum that she has any reason to feel guilty.

So when Queens get parental guilt, that is the one thing they can count on as proof that they aren't shit mums. The guilt is there to tell you, yes you have been busy, or yes you have been tired, or yes you have ordered pizza for three nights in a row and your children have started acting out scenes from Lord of the Flies without having ever seen the movie. But you are still OK, you are not a shit mum because you are feeling parental guilt.

So peel yourself off the couch, change your knickers and boil up some pasta. Because you are an amazing mum.

Embrace your parental guilt, feel grateful that it has come at a time when you needed it but do not dwell on it, do not let it consume you, do not let it make you feel unqueenly.

Queens are too busy changing the world to bother dwelling on parental guilt.

So instead of declaring a war on something that comes so naturally to all good mothers, I have changed my views. Thank you parental guilt for reminding us that we are good mums, now there's the door, see you next time I stuff up, because we both know I will stuff up again soon.

Let guilt be the blessing it was designed to be and not the curse it has become.

I am no expert on raising kids, I was freaked out when I fell pregnant with my first because the only thing I was an expert on was myself.

I feel like every day I wing it, sometimes my kids do something amazing, like fall asleep on the back couch snuggling our two chickens, and sometimes I am shocked that someone so small can be such a big arsehole.

One rule I have stuck with, because I know from personal experience how it feels, is I try (but fail often) to ignore the bad behaviour and reward the good.

I have always seen punishing children as pushing shit up a hill, we punish violence with violence. The children who need attention the most act out the most and in turn are isolated in time-out, self-conscious children are yelled at and embarrassed in public. Disciplining children seems to run parallel with breaking baby hearts, baby hearts should never break.

Being an expert on myself, I know that I need love instead of lectures. When bosses have told me that my work standards are slipping, I slip further, when boyfriends call me psycho, I turn up the psycho. So I have learnt that telling a little girl who has tripped over her brother, stolen his biscuit and nicked off up a tree that she is a naughty girl, is only going to make her throw a stick at you.

My approach to motherhood has taken Bill a lot to get used to. He is more hard arse, he wants to discipline them, he wants them to behave. Of course I do too, I just don't take tantrums personally. I see the pain and rather than exacerbating it, I'm mum, I want to heal it.

THE FIRST BORN

Billie-Violet has shown me that the more trouble she gets in, the more she hates herself. I don't care if my kids stuff up, I don't care if they get detentions, I don't care if they don't go to bed on the dot of eight o'clock, but I do care if they hate themselves. Nothing tears me in half as much as the thought of my child hating herself.

Billie-Violet freaks me out. She's seven and never has there been a better example of a teenage child.

Billie-Violet — who was named after her father and my great-grandmother — is me. Her attitude, her obsession with her friends, her disgruntled rebellion against all things authority, and her early interest in boys — it's all me. And that is what freaks me out. Because she is seven … What is she going to be like at seventeen?

I believe in Billie-Violet, I know that she will do great things but I also know that she will drag me through the mud in my failing attempts to control her. Because she is a fierce heart, answers like "because I said so" don't fly with fierce hearts, answers like "because I'm the adult" don't wash with fierce hearts.

Some call it answering back, others call it questioning everything and I believe that nothing is above questioning.

Being the first born, Billie-Violet is the child who feels the most sorry for herself. She has a deep-seated knowledge that she has lost something, that she deserves more. Because she remembers having more — more of my time, more of her dad's time, more toys, more parcels in the mail. Billie-Violet will always be chasing more.

She is the only one of my children who lost something when she gained siblings and that has given her little life a slightly hard done-by tone, her glass is half empty, because she believes that nobody loved her enough to fill the fucking thing up.

She is that child who leaves a holiday filled with everything she loves and more, in a huff because we didn't go back to the zoo and buy her the meerkat toy that she decided she wants.

It's so easy to get frustrated with her. Not only do we love her to death and back but she single-handedly gets more attention, more time, and more of our decisions are based on her high-maintenance needs than the rest of the kids put together.

Children will teach you how to parent them, they will show you what they need. Sometimes it's an obvious scream and sometimes you need to dig a bit deeper.

Billie-Violet taught me the most valuable lesson I have learnt so far as a mum. She taught me compassion and I thought I had a pretty good grasp on compassion.

Billie-Violet's glass-half-empty attitude needed my compassion. Instead of the natural feeling of anger you get towards someone who is receiving more and satisfied less, she needed my understanding. By getting angry all of the time, all I was doing was validating her belief that life wasn't fair.

So I protect her soul, I try not to get cross with her complaints, I try to understand and empathise with why it might not feel fair.

I reminisce with her about the times when my life didn't feel fair and finally I break through to her, sometimes all we need is to feel understood. Understanding soothes frustration, every time.

Billie-Violet has taught me that empathy and compassion are not black and white, they are not reserved for the disadvantaged and those suffering. Everyone needs them and the special souls who seem like they need them the least are the ones who need them the most.

Billie-Violet is sweet and caring and quirky, she has long, dark, thick hair, green eyes and freckles all over her button nose.

Watching this one grow is interesting, entertaining, inspiring and challenging. I don't really know what I'm doing or where she's taking me, but I know I'm coming. Wherever she goes, I'm coming.

THE LOVE CHILD

Arlo was born without a middle name, then months later I registered his middle name as Love because all I ever saw beaming out of him was love.

My love for Arlo Love has been the most natural and smooth journey I could ever go on, he co-slept from the beginning, he fills me up like a cup of golden warm love that brings with it an easy contentment like nothing I have ever known.

I don't love him the most, obviously I have a favourite child but that position changes every day. One day Billie-Violet is being amazing and she's my favourite and the next Snow's dancing to ads on TV which make her my favourite. Arlo is just easy for me.

Sitting in the doctor's surgery, across the other side of the room, he will be playing with a train track, look up, flick the thick, wavy hair out of his eyes and say "you booful, mum" and you can literally hear all of the Queens' hearts crumble into a million pieces as all around us say "awwwwww". I am done, completed, could die now and everything will be fine.

At four years old, Arlo has big brown eyes, a freckly nose and dark red hair, he has beautiful olive skin, rarely wears a top and never wears shoes. People tell me he's my little surfie hippie child, to me he's just Arlo, natural and loveable.

He's terribly behaved, runs away, throws huge tantrums, steals, lies, you name it, Arlo does it as I blindly carry on, smothering him with kisses and compliments. I can only remember a few times in his life that I have ever gotten mad with him, much to my family's disapproval.

Arlo throws a toy at his dad, his dad gets cross, Arlo runs to me crying, I hug him and tell him it's OK, it was an accident. The whole house shakes their heads at me. I know it's wrong but I can't help it.

One day Billie-Violet and her dad were talking in the kitchen while I was making dinner and I tuned in when I heard Bill talk about Arlo.

Bill: "Our son is a star."

Me: "Ain't that the truth, and he's a warrior and he smells like flowers and he's the cuddliest little bug I've ever met."

Billie-Violet: "Muuumm, we are talking about our solar system!"

Me: "Hmmm … carry on, your dad's right, our sun's a star."

I don't think Arlo will become that kid who aces the NAPLAN tests or wins any scholarships but that just makes him less calculated. He loves his friends, would give them any of his toys, he even wiped his nervous bestie's bum for him on the first day of kindy to save the embarrassment of asking a teacher, and he loves me to death. What more could I ask for?

Move over Bill.

DOUBLE DELIGHT

Being pregnant with the twins shoved my emotions in the dirt, wrung them out and left them in the corner to dry by themselves, still stained with mud.

I was trapped, fat, lonely, heavy, in pain and relying solely on a man who had no time for me. I had nowhere to run to, no plan B, no plan at all. So the birth of the twins will always feel like freedom to me. I had never appreciated freedom before because I knew what being truly trapped felt like.

It was October when they came and the sun was reappearing after a depressing winter, everything seemed to glow. Bill and I would fight and not a single tear would stream down my face, it was like I was protected by a postnatal bubble that I had thought would be depression but it was happiness, because I was free.

Yes, it took forty-five minutes to get everyone in the car, yes I was still very heavy, yes I was totally sleep deprived but I was free. I was no longer in pain, my world was no longer ruled by a man.

I had been so scared throughout my pregnancy, scared of the unknown, scared that I wouldn't be able to handle it. I barely handled one baby, two babies saw me pushed millimetres from the edge and I had a partner for both of them. Now Bill and I barely spoke, I acted brave when people would ask but I was shitting myself daily. I thought my pregnancy was the calm before the storm, little did I know, my pregnancy was the storm.

And then the twinnies were here. To turn my world upside down, two little shiny ones, two little innocent worms who plonked themselves into the middle of my life, entitled as fuck, as if they had always been there. With that special baby superpower of melting my heart with every sound.

I have always been that mum who keeps on keeping on, babies don't get me down. With Billie-Violet, I lost the weight pronto and was back at work by eight months. With Arlo, I lost the weight, put him in daycare and enrolled in uni by the time he was four months old, although once I realised I wasn't into uni, I opened a little hairdressing salon. I thrived on being that mum whose life goes on.

And then the twinnies. I just couldn't lose the weight, I didn't have the drive, I couldn't go back to work because I couldn't afford daycare for them all, nobody I knew could babysit them all for me, I couldn't sleep because it was just so impossible, I couldn't even keep my house clean or cook nice food or get into any sort of a routine, I just couldn't. I had come out of the most depressing ten months of my life and I didn't have the drive to work as hard as someone with four kids needs to work in order to gain order.

And so I welcomed my great surrender ...

I surrendered to everything, getting my body back, trying to work on my marriage, keeping my house clean, working out a sleep routine, the idea of ever working again ... I just let it all go.

And I filled my time with lying on the floor tickling babies, videoing babies, swooning over babies, afternoon walks on the beach, takeaway dinners eaten at the park, long phone calls to my sister. I would spend hours under a tree with my babies, watching Arlo climb the trees, laughing at his jokes and I was truly happy, like really happy, like ecstasy kicking in happy. I was new. Nothing else mattered, just now and these guys.

As my house fell apart, Bill picked up a lot of slack, friends would quickly do the dishes when they came over, I'd put on some music and clean whenever I had a surge of energy to do it. But I realised that nobody was going to die if I went to a new friend's house and left ours a mess, nobody was going to die if I stopped with the gourmet dinners that nobody ate anyway. Nobody was going to die if I cancelled my appointments and just surrendered to the bubble of love that I was lucky enough to be part of.

We were all safe, we were all being looked after, my kids and I were so in love and it wasn't long before Bill joined us again.

My house is still a mess, paint, clothes and toys cover my house, I cook when I want to, I buy sushi when I can't be fucked. For me, now is more important than tomorrow, it's more important than yesterday. Now is all we have and we don't have it forever.

The twins saved my life, they forced me to save my own life.

Snow is my kindest, sweetest, cuddliest baby. She is pure joy, her face lights up at absolutely anybody. I caught her smiling and waving in the mirror, I have numerous photos of her body-slam hugs to the dog, her round belly pokes out as she walks and her thighs and bum are rolly and delicious.

People shouldn't operate heavy machinery when she is around, I shouldn't even use the stove because I cannot be trusted to not drop everything I'm doing at the sight of her chubby little bald head and jump in for a love bomb. She generously hands all of her possessions to the other kids. If someone is tickling Rumi, Snow starts laughing.

Snow was a sound sleeper, a brilliant feeder and despite being a whole head shorter than Rumi, she weighs more than him. A tiny, solid ball of bliss.

Snow loves her food, she loves her family, she loves her teddies, she just loves everything.

Rumi was my most difficult baby, he came out of the womb furiously, not ready, not comfortable. He hated sleeping, spewed up his food. His little face looked so much like a frog that when they handed him to me I wasn't sure whose he was, he looked like Mr Burns from The Simpsons and he was miserable.

I often think about all of those parents who think they must be doing something wrong because their baby screams, spews, doesn't sleep, isn't happy. But having had twins, I know now that some babies just come out like that — Snow was a perfect baby and Rumi was the most troubled. All babies are different so one mum saying you should do it the way she did because her baby slept all night is like telling a horse trainer how you taught your dog to sit. Pointless.

Rumi was miserable for about five months, his little belly wasn't ready, he didn't like sleeping, he cried so much that I found myself daydreaming about Rumi moving in with my mum and even told her that she may need to take him for a couple of nights so that I could get some sleep. Those couple of nights never came, like every exhausted mum, my love for him was stronger than sleep, stronger than sanity — we push through.

And then, like some kind of blossoming flower, Rumi adjusted to life outside of my belly. He started smiling, sleeping and his cheeky little nature exposed itself. Rumi is now my showstopper. He waves at everyone, chats away in his little toddler language, he's so handsome, he sings to me and my heart splats. Like Arlo, he's a brave little risk taker — when Snow's safely in my arms, Rumi's dragging chairs across the floor, climbing on to the bench and navigating his way to a packet of biscuits. Rumi is the glue of the family, he does funny stuff and waits for us to laugh at him, he loves it, loves the limelight. Even on those days where Bill and I can't stand the sight of each other, we bond over how funny Rumi is.

Rumi dominates, Snow loves. Rumi steals, Snow gives. Rumi bashes, Snow cries. Rumi does the funny stuff, Snow laughs.

Together they are my little twin team, I can't believe I ever had a family without them.

NAMING BABIES

Naming babies is my favourite thing to do, every pregnant woman I know unexpectedly receives monthly baby name suggestions from me and not to brag … But I am responsible for quite a few babies' names including my beautiful sister's kids, Valentino and Mattea.

Naming Billie-Violet was the easiest. Bill wasn't sold on the idea of having a baby so I sweetened the deal by offering to name her after him. You see Bill was known as Billy at the time, he is now Bill to minimise confusion and Violet was my beautiful great-grandma's name. She was a bright red lipstick-wearing and unpredictably behaved woman, who had embarked upon a passionate love affair with my great-grandfather. I decided to draw on her as inspiration.

No arguments from Bill or myself.

Arlo was a tough decision, boys are trickier, there is no doubt about it. I had lists of names, I was pregnantly insane so I was confused and started suggesting all sorts of things to Bill — Parley, Oakley, Basil, Arlo. Bill said no to all of them. I then formatted a rule that you are not permitted to dismiss any name choices without offering another.

One night, on Bill's birthday, everyone was drunk except miserable me and they were asking me about baby names, I said I love Arlo and Bill interjected with a "NO".

"Fine," I said. "Give me something better." He thought for a few seconds and responded with "Arn" which was met with silence.

Bill's last name is 'Mahon' pronounced Marn (Arn – Marn) ... I responded with "NO".

Needless to say, when Arlo popped out of my vag and was chucked on my lap after I had shat on my sexy doctor and was having my fanny stitched, Bill wasn't about to argue with anyone and when the nurses asked his name, Bill responded with "Arlo".

Then when the twins came along I was excitedly finding names for them, the boy was going to be Oasias, which reminded me of the ocean that I spend so much time in, and the girl was going to be Viva. I had always loved Viva and was plagued by a bit of naming remorse that I hadn't named Billie-Violet Viva.

Bill agreed until about halfway through when I had second thoughts on Oasias, worried that I was going to look like one of those bogans who pretended to be a hippie because hippie is more acceptable than bogan and an easy disguise. And Bill turned to me and said that in England, Viva is the equivalent of Destiny, a great name ... for a stripper.

Great, back to square one. Until one day I was reading a Rumi quote that read:

"Out beyond the ideas of rightdoing and wrongdoing there is a field. I'll meet you there."

That resonated deeply, I had spent my pregnancy feeling 'wrong' after how I had treated Bill and I just wanted a love that had the strength to rise above right and wrongdoing, so I researched everything I could about this Rumi, a 13th century Persian poet, exactly who I needed at the time. And I decided that I wanted to name my son after him, it felt like a great time to name a little white boy after an inspiring Muslim prophet. Bill surprised me and agreed.

Then I had a name for my little girl but I had to wait until Bill was in the best mood ever, Friday after work. He had a couple of beers and was in fine form and I sprung it on him. "I like the name Snow" … and what the fuck. He agreed. "Yes!! It reminds me of England and Christmas, Snow has a calming effect." I nearly passed out. Usually his name choices were more conservative, I had to cross my fingers that he didn't change his mind.

So I didn't bring it up at all until the babies were out. Naming babies is not one of Bill's passions, it is mine so he won't ask if I don't tell him. The thing is that names are my area, financial structure and building extensions are his, so I don't argue with his choices but when it comes to naming babies … I really do know best.

So on the day that they were sliced out of my stomach, I was on the table, intestines in the doctor's hands, I'm on so many drugs that it looks to me like some nurse with an afro is hanging around my vagina drinking from a straw but it's actually my overgrown pubes and a catheter poking out. The doc asks their names and I mumble "The boy is Rumi and the girl is Snow". Everyone is silent and Bill was just as shocked as them. "What?" he says. "Those names might change, doc," I say. "Um, you agreed to these names Bill, I'm not having a last-min …" "OK, OK," Bill interrupts. "Calm down, they are the names."

If you're having a name debate, remember this. Nobody has more pull than a freshly birthed mum. Patience is the key.

A day later I got a message from my cousin that said "Great names Con!! I particularly like what you did with Snow, her full name is Snow-Man!!"

Yes … Bill's last name is pronounced Marn. Snow Marn. Name fail.

But she was already the perfect little Snowdrop bundle of Snow pea joy that I just couldn't change it. I am working on changing the pronunciation of Bill's last name to the way that it's spelt, Mahon. He's not buying it. Face palm.

WHO DO YOU WANT YOUR CHILDREN TO BE?

As Queens we put so much pressure on ourselves, we are told that to be a good mother you have to love every single fucking second of it, be grateful for your fertility, be happy that your children are healthy and living in a land of wealth and abundance, clean that huge floating shit out of the bath with a massive grin on your face because that is "motherhood". We, Western women, are living with great privilege — to be anything other than grateful and appreciative is a massive kick in the face to the rest of the world.

Some days of motherhood can go and fuck themselves with a bottle of cider and a nice big fatly rolled spliff on your back deck, once the four ungrateful little sods you have somehow raised are finally a-fucking-sleep.

It can be so tough that it's funny. I know I'm not the only one who has laughed while hiding in the laundry eating a piece of chocolate that was promised to their greedy little spawn for eating their dinner. Sorry sweetheart, the dog must have eaten it.

I think one of the main reasons that we are so overwhelmed is the pressure we put on ourselves, everything has been upped to unreachable degrees nowadays. When I was young, we were jumping on trampolines and playing with our dogs until the sun went down. Now it's not uncommon for me to meet a lady who tells me that her son speaks three languages, is a blackbelt in karate, has two degrees — one of which is medicine — and his pilot's licence. And he's only four!

My children aren't particularly amazing at much, they aren't the most athletic or academic or creative or polite children in the world. But Billie-Violet can climb damn high in a tree and Arlo has a unique ability to fall off playground equipment without getting too hurt. The only thing they are the absolute best at being is themselves.

I learnt the hard way that encouraging anything else of them is only setting them up for failure.

When Billie-Violet was in kindy, I was busy working full time. I was under this weird illusion that once my kids were in school, I would find myself with all this free time, free time that I chose to spend working. (I'm not sure if that really constitutes free time but as anyone who has ever been a stay-at-home mum will tell you, working is pretty freeing.) It was my first introduction to being a mother with a child in the education system and I found that between dropping off, making school lunches, getting her clothes ready, staying with her in class while she wrote out her name or settled on the mat, doing her hair, picking her up and doing her reading, I wasn't actually left with any free time at all.

Some times I think about what I want my children to become, they are on their own journey and I am here to open their minds, it's my job to guide and protect them.

I want them to feel compassion. Feeling compassion is as much a gift to you as it is to the person you feel it for.

I want them to acknowledge their privilege. Privilege isn't a gift, it's a responsibility. My children were born in a Western world country, they are immunised, they are educated and they are safe. That is a privilege. To honour this privilege, I want dedicated world savers. If you don't use your privilege to help the less fortunate and bridge the divide, it is wasted on you.

I want them to feel and believe in freedom. There are so many trapped souls in this world. I want my children to know who they are and be open to change, life paths twist and turn, and belief systems do complete U-turns. I want my children's lives to be in a constant state of growth and evolution.

I want them to feel love. Real love, companionship, I want them at least once in their lives to feel a love that runs deeper than fit bodies with shaggy hair, a love deeper than blue eyes. I want them to feel a love that I feel when I hold them, a love that challenges the terms "me and you".

My children won't achieve any of this unless they completely love themselves. So my job is to raise them with a deep and rich understanding of self-acceptance.

My dad taught me one thing, that copying is more effective than teaching lessons. He went through his life listening to me, listening to my stories and loving me. He never sat me down to teach me anything and yet somehow I learnt so much from him.

So I adopt his methods to get my message of self-acceptance through to my darling children. I accept myself in every way possible every day in front of them to show them how to love yourself, in the hope that they will copy me and everything they want to be in this world, every little decision they make will be supported by an outpouring of love. Every little fuck-up will be dusted off promptly, every little letdown will be a learning curve, every little journey will be one of purpose because they love themselves.

That is my hope for my children.

LET'S HEAR IT FOR BOREDOM

A kid with an activity to do is one thing — that kid doing that activity. A kid with nothing to do is a million things: a pirate, a doctor, an astronaut, a fairy who lives under a mushroom, a mermaid ... Anything.

We spend so much of our lives scared that our kids will get bored. The guilt I have felt when I was too pregnant to go out, or working too hard at home, letting my children get bored. But boredom is a workout for the imagination, the more bored the child, the more elaborate the fantasy.

I spent a lot of time alone as a child, my sister moved to Melbourne with my dad, my mum worked full time. At the age of ten, I had a key to my house and would walk home after school to set up my stage in my bedroom and begin my Wembley Stadium performance, or set up my students of teddies and pillows and begin my science lesson as Miss Hall.

When I was bored, I was anything I wanted to be. I would dress up in my mum's clothes, stare at myself in the mirror and put on accents. I'd write and draw and hang out outside, sitting in my mulberry tree, my imagination completely took over. I still to this day zone out all the time, make up scenarios in my head, plan things, mentally change things that I don't like.

Boredom will always be the great brain expander in my eyes, so when my kids are hassling me, constantly throwing in their favourite line "I'M BORED MUUUUUUM!!!!" instead of finding them some activity to distract them from their own imagination, I'm that bitch mum who yells back "GOOD!" Because they need it, tapping into that imagination saved me and you can't tap into it until boredom completely takes over.

For a girl who took very little from her school education, I certainly am grateful that my brain had a chance to explore the world when I got home.

There is a time for boredom.

SAY NO TO BULLYING

One thing I will never take lightly is bullying. Bullying has been handled with the same approach as sexual abuse, where women have been taught safety precautions. Therefore if one has failed to follow the guidelines and is assaulted, society can indirectly blame her, the victim, for not taking responsibility for her own safety.

Bullying is the same, we teach our children to ignore bullies, we teach our children to talk to teachers, talk to their parents, we teach them how to counteract bullying every day. Yes, this is vital, as I want my children to come to me straight away if they are bullied.

But the real problem is being ignored. What are the bullies being taught? What are the parents of the bullies doing? Because people can freely admit that their children are being bullied but nobody wants to talk about the fact that their children are bullying, it's shameful.

What if we removed the shame? What if we all accepted that becoming a bully is easy enough to do. I have a seven-year-old girl who has bullied the absolute fuck out of Arlo, for such a delightful little strawberry, Billie-Violet can get her mean girl on at the drop of a hat. Especially if she has friends over. Pack mentality is rife amongst children.

So I won't judge the woman whose kid is caught bullying but I will ask what are we going to do about it?

Because bullying needs a major crackdown. Major.

- Suicide is the third leading cause of death amongst young people.

- Bullying victims are up to nine times more likely to commit suicide.

- For every Australian suicide, there are up to 100 attempts.

- Studies show that at least half of the suicides in young people are a result of bullying.

What are we going to do about it? If the statistics of getting shot by a gun when you walk into a schoolyard were that high, none of us would be expected to send our kids to school. Yet we are told to send them, we are told that they will be OK.

I am that mum whose children are climbing on top of the fridge while I'm drinking tea. I am that mum whose kids are in trouble for swearing and I try not to laugh. I am that mum whose kids are up at 10pm painting a beautiful picture of a colourful frog.

But I am also that mum who jumped up at a dinner party, threw my kids in the car and drove them home where I made them watch me throw every single Christmas present they got in the bin because they joined in picking on my friend's kid.

I say no.

Children who engage in bullying need major consequences, they need to be shown exactly what they have done, they have to be forced into the victim's home, they should have to clean that victim's Lego up for hours, they need to look that victim in the eyes and listen to them explain how hurt they are.

Children are too young to reasonably understand what they are doing, our job is to show them.

It is our job as parents to stop our children from bullying. We need to intervene. We need to drag our children to the police station, to the principal's office, we need to say no.

Parents of the victims need to say no. If the school ignores you, stick banners all over the place, start online petitions, hold meetings.

I will not let my child bully or be bullied. If I have to move away to the desert, I will. I will not let my child be a victim and end up dead, nor will I let my child have to live, for the rest of their lives, knowing they are the reason that another child is dead.

LOVE MY WAY

I remember being a teenager and watching a family friend, Joan, raise her daughter, Alexis. Joan was a recovered drug addict, who I suspected still dabbled. She was a wild party animal and borderline alcoholic and had also been a prostitute. She had the kindest of hearts but couldn't seem to figure life out or maybe she had it figured out and hated what she saw so she hid in an alternative lifestyle.

Joan did whatever Alexis said. I stayed with them when I was fifteen and Alexis was two. Alexis completely put me off having children, she was demanding and rude, she slept in her mum's bed, tore the house up and Joan would just laugh at her wildness. Joan had her old loser mates over, they would drink and smoke weed and party all night, Alexis had no bed time, she crashed when she felt like it.

Once at 2am, I was woken up on the couch by Joan sneaking out and climbing the back fence. I asked her what the hell she was doing, she reappeared with the neighbour's dog and told me that Alexis had woken up in the middle of the night and wanted to cuddle a puppy, so Joan went and got her one. As a judgmental teenager, my thought process was something like: "Wow, Joan is seriously fucking Alexis up, she's going to be a spoilt brat forever, no hope, such shit parenting."

Throughout Alexis' life she must have moved States five times — whenever Joan met a new boyfriend, they moved for him. They never had any money and Joan was all over the place, the only thing for sure was that Joan loved Alexis.

Do you want to know where Alexis is now? After receiving the dux award at the end of high school, she was awarded a scholarship to study medicine at the most prestigious university in WA, she didn't accept because she wanted to spend a year volunteering in India. When you talk to Alexis, you are talking to the most beautiful, understanding, caring women possible. She is stunning and cool and makes you want to be her, she's authentic and genuine. If I ever wanted any of my kids to be like someone else, it would be her.

Alexis and Joan are still really close, I often think of Joan and remind myself that my kids will be fine, they survive on my love.

When in doubt, choose love.

STOP WORRYING

I have a recurring thought since becoming a mum, "I'm fucking them up". With my laziness and my fights with Bill, my working or my not working, my short temper, my relaxed nature, my maths that is so bad I can't even help a seven-year-old with her homework, and my inability to come up with a meal that anyone actually eats.

You will lose your shit, you will do things you are not proud of, you will stuff up big time — all the time — while rarely you will have an incredible victory.

But remember that doubting yourself and being weighed down by parental guilt won't do your children any favours, while self-love will give them something to aspire towards.

- Keep them in touch with nature, the ocean heals, the bush inspires, animals teach.
- Don't reward dobbing.
- Encourage softness, children are soft and strong, the word weakness should only ever be used to describe coffee.
- Don't bully your children into not bullying, show them first hand the effects of bullying.
- Don't give too many fucks about swearing for emphasis, that's passion. Don't tolerate swearing at someone.
- You can't ruin your children with compassion, you can't ruin anything with compassion. Choose compassion.

I once went to a Maggie Dent seminar, she is the total guru of parenting and somehow manages to make you love your kids more leaving her talks than you did when you walked in. I love everything that she says and does for children, she is a rational voice for the irrational kids.

I have never, ever forgotten these life-changing words that she ended the seminar with:

"As parents, we keep a lot of our special things locked away for important house guests, the good crockery and the expensive plates. The kids tend to trash everything so when important people come over we like to add a bit of special.

I worked at a funeral home for a few years, consoling parents on losing their children, talking them through the confronting reality of losing a child forever.

After spending a large part of your career in such an unimaginable position, you come to some pretty life-changing conclusions.

Raising our children is a privilege denied to many, every day that we spend with them is a blessing, no matter how hard or testing, it is a blessing.

Your children are the most important people to ever walk through your front door. The important house guests are right in front of you.

Use the good crockery."

— Maggie Dent

At least once every couple of months that story comes back to me, my kids are my important house guests.

Just keep on Queening on, stop worrying about the small shit. They are humans, some days they win a running race and share their lunch with a kid who's being bullied and some days they watch TV for four hours and get caught shoplifting. Our kids are on a journey too, they will be OK. You are not fucking them up.

LEAVE THE MESS

There comes a time in every Queen's life when they need to redefine the term "clean".

Because if you have children or a job or a life or a creative passion, you simply will not have time to have a clean house and stay happy. Something has to give and that something has to be cleanliness.

Too often Queens choose happiness as their sacrifice.

I am a messy person. Don't get me wrong, I love a clean house. When I come home and someone has cleaned my house for me, I happy dance pelvic thrust through the rooms.

But keeping it at that standard is virtually impossible. I hate cleaning more than most, almost as much as I hate exercise, but at least when I exercise (rarely) I don't have four little saboteurs following me, giving me back every kilo I lose. Which is exactly what I have when I try to clean. Little life ruiners, stalking me, messing up clean washing piles, throwing food on freshly mopped floors, smearing poo leakage on clean bed sheets … It's the most depressing and unrewarding act of our time.

There came a time when I realised a clean house wouldn't bring me happiness, in fact it brings me stress. The pressure of maintaining the cleanliness turns me into an arsehole who yells at her kids non-stop to stop making a goddamn mess, which is precisely what children are designed to do, so I gave up.

I am now the proud owner of the messiest house that you will ever walk into. Bill, the clean freak, has required complete reprogramming to avoid a panic attack every time he walks into our Lego-filled, clothes kicked off, dishes piling up, cubbies galore, headquarters.

Most weeks my dirty undies spend more time on our bathroom floor than our bathmat does. Bill freaks out, he calls them my experiment and believes that one day they will grow legs and drag themselves to the washing machine. It may happen.

Messy is the new clean. If my house doesn't stink and there is a clean cup for my tea that means my house is clean.

Yes, we still need to do housework, Bill does the clothes washing, I do the dishes and we kind of just get the rest of it done every now and then. But it's not my priority, it comes after everything else — after happiness, after love, after reading stories and painting pictures. Housework in my house has been put in its place, at the bottom of the agenda.

This loud and colourful and relaxed home of ours oozes happiness, comfort and love. Looking at every house I have ever entered, I can say honestly that the inhabitants of the messiest ones are the happiest.

I choose happiness.

CHAPTER 8
Growing Up Constance

My childhood was nothing out of the ordinary, not to me anyway. I had a mum, a dad, a big sister whom I idolised and would happily tie myself to a train track or fart in front of guests if she suggested that it could possibly crack a smile on her face.

My mum kicked my dad to the curb when I was six months old and he brokenheartedly returned to Melbourne, leaving my sister and me to live with my mum in Perth.

My mum, despite enjoying a couple of wild years of heroin use when she met my dad, was deep down a shit-together kind of woman.

With a very resilient exterior, she was happy to cut loose anyone who was dragging her down. I probably learnt that when my dad left and definitely learnt it when a dog so much as coughed and bought himself a one-way car ride to the vet. Most of our pets lived in anxiety, knowing that if they showed an ounce of weakness it was green needle time.

Thank fuck none of these rules applied to her children, we were the exception and received nothing but compassion and love. I have been ill and a fuck-up and drained the life out of my mum and she is yet to get rid of me.

My mum believed in working full time because even though after paying for daycare she was only bringing home an extra $70 a week than the single-mother pension, she was convinced that that $70 was all the difference we needed. My mother was born to a rogue member of an affluent family, her mother who I never met was said to be slightly insane and incredibly warm, a description I'd be honoured to have on my own gravestone.

So while my mother's childhood was interesting, she was still from a high-society family and held a tight grip to her strong connections with the class system. So she worked as a secretary and we went from one falling-down rental to another in one of the most expensive suburbs in Perth, because this is what my mum believed was the best life she could offer her children.

Stella and I didn't care about the shitty rentals, we took moving house in our stride. Some nights we ate baked beans for dinner, some nights my mum would apologise that all we could afford was pancakes. Like any normal kids, we were stoked since "poor food" tended to be pretty cool. When she was paid, she would cook anything from curries to roasts and we would eat it all. How she managed to get her girls to love the food she cooked baffles me now as a mother.

Sisters are the absolute shit. Mine is my life and without her, I'm not me.

She's the one person I can tell anything to and know through and through that her intentions for me are always good.

She brags about my success and scoops up my failures. Stella, who is three years older than me, hasn't ever competed with me or taken any joy in my failures or even thrown me a cheap "I told you so". She's just there, like some sort of big sister mascot, my one consistent, my rock.

Stella wasn't always this holy all-loving sister, she was a massive bitch when we were little. She told me to jump and I would ask how high, she would get me to massage her and her friends when they had sleepovers and I'd happily do it, without a return massage, just so I could hang out with her. Whatever nasty little jokes she let me be the butt of, I'd gratefully lap up.

Stella was the high-maintenance, high-achieving, highly strung sister. My mum would drop us both off to see my dad and by home time when mum returned, Stella would have her bag packed, hair done and be sitting waiting to be collected. I would be in the mud, watering a tree with my nappy around my feet.

We have always been chalk and cheese. Stella was a bookworm, a straight-A student. I would pretend to read and get embarrassed when I realised my book was upside-down. Stella has always been a clean freak, I have always been feral. Opposites since we were born, she was stick thin and I was a Buddha.

When I was eight, we moved to Melbourne for six months. We lived with my dad and then moved to my aunty's house and my mum met us shortly after. She tried to find work there and put us in a local school. I loved it,

Stella loved it but after a while of not having any work or being around her family, my mum decided it was time to move home.

Nobody really bothered to keep me in the loop, I just sort of followed and didn't complain too much. I think that's part of being the easy-going sibling, people tend to forget to tell you anything. It's not like I would complain, when I was with my sister everything was cool, she was my idol so I didn't need much else.

The day that we moved back to Perth was possibly one of the most confusing and miserable days of my life. I remember putting my bag in the car, saying my usual teary goodbye to my dad, he would try to make me smile, always succeeding but never taking away the sorrow. I got in the car, mum fastened my seatbelt and got into the passenger seat, god knows who was driving us … and then it hit me. Stella wasn't coming. I had heard people talking about how much she liked the school there, maybe they had tried to tell me that she wasn't coming home but I had switched off — I tend to switch off when I don't want to know things. I will never forget the greyness that washed over me as we pulled out of my aunty's driveway in Essendon that day. Stella didn't make eye contact with me and I settled into a feeling that I'd learn to get used to — glumness.

That was the beginning of life as a duo, just me and mum. We would sign up for a whole year in a rental place and even though commonsense tells me that four seasons must have passed, all I can remember is winter. I have vivid memories of getting off buses in the dark and in the rain, after after-school care, walking for a kilometre back to our flat and getting splashed by puddles from the passing traffic. All the while, we wouldn't say anything to each other. Mum must have been shattered after a day talking to customers as a receptionist and then a long trip to pick me up on public transport. Those splashes felt like big fat fuck yous from all those happy families who could afford warm cars.

Sometimes when I'm consumed with parent guilt, for having so many children and not having enough time or money to do the things that I always wanted to do with my kids, I think back to that time. I think about all the joy that having a sibling meant to me and I realise that I faced some really intense things as a kid with my sister around. Mum's boyfriend pulling a knife on my uncle, my mum having a seizure after an allergic reaction to some anti-depressants, my dad's house getting raided by undercover cops — and yet all of this was water off a duck's back because I had my sister with me and we just kept on playing. Yet when she was gone, getting splashed by passing traffic was enough to push me into a deeper, darker depression.

So I forgive myself for being spread too thin, for having too many kids, I ignore the "I hate Arlos!!!" and the "Billie ruined everythings!!!!" that I constantly hear because I am giving them the greatest gifts of their lives — they just don't know it yet.

Distance didn't kill my relationship with Stella, we remained close. She would send me clothes that I would squeeze into and I would call her most nights. Surprisingly, she was raised by dad and I was raised by mum yet I ended up taking after dad, being an artist, a mess freak, a drinker, and Stella inherited mum's cleanliness and organisational skills.

When I moved to Melbourne, I moved in with Stella and we have been as close as close ever since.

Stella doesn't drink which meant she could pick me up outside a nightclub at 3am, when I was completely off my head wearing her clothes that I hadn't asked to borrow and had now christened with a cigarette burn. I'd promise myself every time that I wouldn't call her, that I'd save enough money for a cab and she would warn me every time that if I did call her, she wouldn't come. But sure enough, I'd borrow someone's phone, call her and whisper in my creepiest voice "Steeeeeeeelllllllaaaaaaaa" to which she would sleepily ask "where are you then?" And no matter how angry and tired she was, I'd always be able to make her laugh in the car on the way home, just before passing out.

Now we are both married, we both have kids – she's given me a niece and a nephew who I love with a special part of my heart that's reserved just for them. Our lives are such opposites, people are always shocked to hear that we are not only sisters but as close as we are.

Stella's house is an immaculate, three-storey place with city views. It's always clean and she cooks her kids food from scratch. She dresses her children in designer clothes and keeps them to a routine. My house is a tiny pigsty with a million people living in it. I buy as much ready-made food as possible, we don't wear shoes and we have no routines.

And do you know what? That's what I love about her, she's shown me that you can have a perfect house and not be an arsehole, she's shown me that kids who wear two-hundred-dollar shoes aren't any less kind or adventurous than my barefoot warriors. Most importantly, I have realised that those whose lives look perfect aren't. Stella is a really private woman, she isn't like me who'll cry to a checkout chick about a fight with Bill. Stella has personal boundaries, she tells me when she's upset or when things aren't going well, she just doesn't broadcast it. She may have a routine but that routine consists of her beautiful boy falling asleep in her arms every night, so I'm learning that the routine mums who bake and don't have new dreadlocks appearing daily are still human and that has made me so protective of the "perfect mother" because I used to judge that bitch. I used to stick my nose up at the woman who looked like everything was perfect as if her whole existence was one big slap in my face. But it's not. The perfect mums are struggling and learning and fucking up just as much as we are. Sure Stella isn't drinking a bottle of whiskey at night but she's got her stuff going on — we all do.

Stella has been the one thing in my life that I can trust emphatically. She doesn't bitch about me — if anyone else does, she exhibits the rage — and she's my biggest fan. Since I was a kid, she'd cry laughing at my jokes, I would imitate mum's laugh or a teacher's walk and I could have her on the ground laughing. She shares the things that I write, she called me crying the first time that I had an article written about me and I didn't know if I was happier for me or happier for her to finally have her love for my writing validated.

I wouldn't be who I am today if I didn't have Stella, she has given me a sense of security since I was a kid and that security has given me my no-fucks attitude. Late rent, parking fines, angry principals ... I've kind of always known that I was going to be OK and a lot of that's been because I had my sister by my side. Nothing feels safer for me than having Stella in my life, I have always known that I could fall but I'd never smash. Stella doesn't let me smash.

That's why sisters are the absolute shit.

The years between my sister moving away and my mum remarrying were the loneliest and most character building of my life.

I was nine years old when my mum took me out of after-school care and gave me my own house key. We had moved into a rental that was an hour's walk from my school, I hated after-school care so much, it felt like kindergarten. When all of my friends and their brothers and sisters were greeted at the school gates by loving mums and dads, I absolutely hated the bus that I had to climb into and sing stupid fucking songs on my way to a place that would treat me like I was three.

Mum decided to let me make my own way home where she would meet me after work at six.

Every week I would desperately try to plan play dates at other kids' houses, smiling at their mums hoping to hear those glorious words, "wanna come over, Con?" I'd invite myself when I didn't get graced with one and a lot of the time I pulled it off and my mum would pick me up from their houses that night on her way home from work. I remember once a friend's dad looked at me as I walked out of the school grounds towards him and before I had the chance to even ask, he snapped "not today, Connie" and I shrivelled. Back into my box, off to walk all the way home with a pretty much confirmed knowledge that I was an unlovable little pile of poo. It's funny how one small comment from an adult who was clearly just having a bad day can stay with a kid forever. I really must remember that.

I became a timid kid, a shadow of the ballsy outspoken child I was once praised for being.

There was only one route I could take to walk home after school due to an old closed-down drive-in theatre near my house. So most days I'd begin my walk, for the first twenty minutes I'd dread knowing that I was about to pass the high school kids at a bus stop and they would tease me because my school skirt came down to my ankles. After cringing through that, my heart would start pounding over a dog who would snarl at me showing his teeth, even though I'd purposely walk on the other side of the road.

194

Once I had survived these first two obstacles, I would start to freak out about an intellectually and physically disabled man who lived on my street who would wait until he saw me and chase me most days. I would have to run to my house and then he would turn back. He scared the absolute shit out of me.

My mum did everything she could to make me feel better, she went to the dog owner's house and insisted that they lock their dog inside after school hours, she had the disabled man's carer come over to explain to me that he was harmless and only chased me to say hi. But nothing anyone could say or do would stop me from hating the world and seeing it as an evil war zone wanting to swallow me.

Once I got home, I would watch movies that I had recorded. They weren't even children's movies, I have no idea why I watched these boring films over and over again. At one point I watched City Slickers with Billy Crystal every day after school with the curtains drawn and the lights off and I can't for the life of me tell you why.

I was bored, lonely and scared. If a door-to-door salesman knocked on my door, I would hide under the table or call my mum at work and pretend someone was trying to break in.

One night while at a Chinese karaoke restaurant, one of my mum's friends asked me how I was, I did the polite thing and said "good thanks". She responded by saying: "Oh to be a kid, you guys have nothing in the world to worry about. You're very lucky."

Even at that young age, I wasn't angry at her ignorance, I felt like explaining to her that I do have things to worry about, in fact I probably worry more than she does. Everyone's problems are relevant to their own lives, mine might seem irrelevant to you but I can tell you now that if something is worrying someone enough that it depresses them, then it's relevant. I didn't say that, I didn't feel worthy of giving an adult a life lesson, but I took the lesson on myself and at that karaoke restaurant, slurping bits of lemonade through the ice, I told myself that nothing that upsets or hurts anyone is ever insignificant.

My life got better when my mum found a rental right next to my school, next door to my close friend, down the road from my best friend. My house became the cool place to hang out because there wasn't any adult supervision so I was surrounded by friends, my front yard was the hang-out spot, neighbours and friends were always there in my trees, on my trampoline. I even had a tree house that we all flocked to after school to bitch about boys and compare new pubes. I was so happy, all the time. It had taken me a while to get there but I was well and truly there.

LOST AND FOUND

When I was fifteen, I went completely off the rails. Not in a booze and drugs and sex kind of way but in a troubled youth kind of way. I was looking for trouble, I wanted adventure and developed a taste for danger and risk taking.

I met a boy at a local dance party, he was into his graffiti and sniffing butane (which is pretty much like sniffing petrol). His friends were older than me, all over eighteen, and into petty crimes such as robbing laundromats to pay for spray paints and shit to sniff before they passed out on the side of the road. Some were into heavier drugs such as heroin. I wasn't, I was just there for the thrill.

I couldn't see it for what it was, I had no idea what I was doing, but they included me and they were exciting. My family hated it, they hated the way

I looked trailing beside a pack of thugs, in my big Adidas jumper, trying to fit in. But no matter how many times my mum begged me to come home, I wouldn't.

Even though the boy and I broke up after a few weeks, I remained friends with the girls he knew. These kids didn't have bed times, in fact they didn't have homes and all crashed at some random house. Now I was doing the same, sleeping on floors, finding money to afford booze. Someone would get arrested, someone would get beaten up — I had never realised how exciting being a "dero" really was.

One night we were doing the rounds in Fremantle, loitering, hanging around fast-food places, train stations, fuck knows what we were really doing. Someone was always waiting for someone, to bring back something so that we could do something.

A group of Aborigines approached us, nobody fucked with them since they were the best fighters and travelled in large groups. They seemed interested in hanging out. Although I was on edge — they looked really tough, really scary — I was flattered that they befriended me and invited me to come for a walk with them. I was too scared to say no, and also intrigued since if they really did want to be friends, I'd be rolling with the toughest of the tough.

Then they asked me for money. I didn't have a cent, had no job, wasn't on any kind of government youth allowance. When I told them I was broke, they got me to ask people for money and bring it to them. They took me to some pretty dark parts of a usually buzzing town and pointed to random people, telling me to ask them for money while they waited. I did as I was told, I even remember telling one couple that I needed money because I was petrified that these people would beat the shit out of me if I didn't give them some. They asked me if I was OK before handing me some coins.

The truth is I didn't know if I was OK. I wasn't going home because I was bored there, but I was scared shitless here and didn't fit in anywhere. On my mission to find somewhere to belong, I was completely lost.

I handed the money over and did it a few more times, I think this crew started to realise that people weren't giving much money over to me just because I was a white girl and soon grew bored of making me collect money.

Instead they told me to follow them up an alleyway, it led to a dark park near the back of the town library. It must have been midnight on a Friday night, there were people around, just not where I was being taken.

I knew that something was going to happen to me, so I began to back off. They noticed that I was trying to get away and I still thought that my best bet was to be as nice as I could to them. Looking back, my best bet would have been to run, as fast as I could.

As we walked, some of them behind me, some in front, all looking around to see if anyone was watching us, I offered them the watch my mum had given me. They ignored my offer and ushered me around the corner where they told me to stand against the wall.

"Please," I begged. "I haven't done anything, please just let me go."

"No," barked one who appeared to be the leader. "You are an ignorant little white cunt" and she punched me square in the face.

I cried and put my hands over my face. There were six of them, I had no option but to scrunch up into a ball and pray for it to be over.

Only the pack leader didn't like the idea of that. "Put your guards down," she snapped.

"What?" I had no idea what guards are, I have never been a fighter.

"Your hands, pull them down or we'll slit your throat."

So I moved my hands down to my side and gave them free range to go to town on my face, one after another they punched me, my head bashing into the brick wall behind me with every blow. A guy came over to me, I thought he might help but he smashed me right in the face too.

I was covered in blood as they kicked my body, slapped my face and asked me to look at them as they punched me. I felt like I was in a movie, watching somebody else defencelessly get the shit beaten out of them. Finally, one of the girls spat on me as they all laughed and walked off.

Eventually, I peeled myself off the ground and looked around for someone to help me. Men clutched on to their drunk girlfriends as they passed by. Is this what it's like to be a street kid? Nobody cares about you? Is this what it's like to be underprivileged? My whole life I knew that someone would help if I needed it. But now, I didn't look like a girl from a good neighbourhood, so they just wanted to keep walking, scared of what you might bring into their lives.

Now petrified of Aborigines, I was looking for a white person to pick me up, to help me, to keep me safe. But none were interested. I tried to hitchhike but nobody was stopping.

All of the sudden, out of nowhere, I was grabbed. Two hands on my shoulders and I glimpsed an Aboriginal man's face and my heart skipped a beat as I tried to shrug away from him.

"Girl, you're in a bad way," he said.

I nodded.

"Where ya going?"

I told him I was off to a friend's flat in Mosman Park.

He hailed me a car, took me to the gate and helped me up the stairs, rang the bell and as the door opened, he was gone.

I do remember him advising me to take better care of myself, that I was better than this. I knew then I would never forget his beautiful kind face, because of how much his care meant to me.

The next day, there was a knock at my friend's door, it was my mum, stepdad and baby brother. My mum wasn't taking no for an answer, she had bought me a one-way ticket to Melbourne and said I had to go before I lost everything. I looked around at all of my "friends". They didn't care about me nor did they have the privilege of a family who wanted to keep them safe. I saw sadness in them and realised it wasn't sadness at the loss of my friendship.

So I reluctantly went.

I always think about what leaving did to me. Off-the-rails teenagers, those who won't listen to anybody and are putting their own safety at risk, need to be removed and for as long as it takes to sever ties, as long as it takes to rewire their confused minds. I hated the first month of being away, I wanted my friends, still craving the thrill of it...

The second month I got used to it. The third month I missed my mum but was scared to come home because I didn't want to see any of the kids I'd been cruising around with. Four months later, I was ready to go home. I went straight back into school and never ever saw any of those kids again. Space heals.

If I am ever faced with any of my kids going down this road, space will be the first place I turn to.

Years later, I would cut that beautiful Aboriginal man's hair and get to know his family, while I cut his five kids and wife's hair too. He is a hard-working man who loves his family. He has never drank alcohol and doesn't do any drugs yet they live below the poverty line.

Sometimes I see him catching the bus to work in the mornings, we share a wave but a strong sense of injustice washes over me as I drive past in my twenty-thousand-dollar car, all of my kids well dressed. To say that the divide doesn't exist is naive. His is the face that saved me — the face that I remember when I hear racist slang being thrown around.

He saved me that night, at a time that I dipped myself into that world only to be plucked out by my world. Nobody ever plucked him out. He never made the bad choices that I made, he has also never had the same opportunities in life as I have.

Yet he didn't see "white girl", he didn't see "spoilt privileged girl", he saw "broken girl" and he fixed her.

And the day came that I, as an adult, as a woman who isn't scared of much, saw one of the girls who hurt me that night — I still have a scar on the inside of my lip and on my chin. To be so savvy with violence at such a young age … What the fuck was their normal?

What opportunities were they offered in this life?

She was sitting at a bus stop, covered in the spray paint she was sniffing through a brown paper bag. My anger and fear washed away. I was only sad that she wasn't offered any opportunities at all.

This has to change.

FAMILY TIES

My family was gossiped about a lot, I was used to it. Try living in a posh suburb and having two former heroin addicts as your parents, including one pretty damn good-looking single mother who loved nothing more than to go out, get boozed and pick up a new lover, and you get used to whispers.

Whispers have always shadowed me, like some sort of imaginary friend that I neither dislike nor am interested in. I have learnt to coexist with them without really thinking about it.

Until once when telling me about someone's divorce problems, my best friend of twenty-five years said to me: "She's just really worried about the divorce affecting her family and friends, she doesn't want to let everybody down."

This shocked me, I could not grasp how anybody could be swayed by "other people" when making a life-changing decision. "Really? Who gives a flying fuck what anybody else thinks, that's mental. It's her life, she needs to just run with whatever she wants to do, not what's expected of her."

To which my best friend offered a reflection that only best friends could: "Con, I love you but you have a really unique ability to not give a fuck about what people say. You don't really look back and for some reason you don't really care what people think of you. Not everyone's like that. It's not mental, it's just her."

That surprised me, I mean I did care what people thought of me, I thought I did anyway. Like if someone says my breath stinks, I cringe all day and try to get over it but the brain that loves to torture me reminds me of it constantly. I just don't really care about how my life affects other people, it's my life, and I'm a headstrong woman whose balls are bigger than most men you know.

I suppose people don't really bother to inform you when you have "disappointed" them. Or maybe I never disappointed either of my parents. After being asked to leave three different high schools, they had incredibly low expectations of me to the point that when I got a job at the supermarket swiping barcodes, my mum bought me a new outfit and insisted the whole extended family went out to celebrate.

I guess people talking about me is still there, still an imaginary bestie that I inherited from a unique situation in an otherwise stuck-up bitch of a town. Always been there, always will, no fucks given.

Of course, not having a dad around really sucks. You don't have strong memories or consciously know exactly what you're missing, you just crave a man, one to talk to on the phone all the time, a man whose memory blends in and out of reality, dreams and stories you have been told. At first I try to distinguish what was a dream and then other times I don't see the point — I prefer to leave it as a blur.

I remember fantasising about my dad. I wanted a hero, who could make me a hero too.

In my eyes he looked like Elvis, actually in reality he looked a bit like Elvis, which was kind of weird until rockabillies made a comeback and then it was kind of cool. I used to lie awake at night and imagine my dad surprising me at school pick-up with a box full of new puppies. That would show everyone, prove that I had a really cool Elvis-esque dad who loved me and just to make everyone really fucking jealous we had puppies, instant class hero. BAM.

I learnt young that my dad was the free-loving hippie artist type, rich in love and poor in cash. Love is worth more than millions but love doesn't buy you return airfares to Perth — or puppies. So my fantasies went on to remain just that, a dream of a more heroic world … with him in it.

I can now quite confidently refer to this as my very first affirmation that a man would fix all of my problems.

My mum is so irrational, she shoots from the hip and if anyone hurts her feelings, she's like a wounded animal and attacks everyone. I would say that 50 per cent of the time we are talking and 50 per cent of the time we're not.

She is, however very forgiving, so even though she will call you up out of the blue and tell you how much of a dickhead you are and how much she can't stand your husband and how you are both ruining your children, she will call you back in a week and tell you that she forgives you for your wrongdoings towards her.

I think it's funny and have learnt during my thirty-three years that my mum is a mental case and I don't take any of it personally. Bill is still halfway through his 'learning to deal with my mum' course and to be honest I don't think he's interested in passing. He still takes her outbursts personally.

I forgive her because I love her. She is smart and caring, so caring, there is nothing in the world that she wouldn't do for her children.

My mum was always the beautiful one, everywhere she went people told her how beautiful she was, she modelled and worked in clothing stores. She was short though, too small to really be a successful model and far too sensitive. At fifty-three, she still generates a lot of attention, partly for being a shameless flirt and partly for being an argumentative psycho.

In the 1970s, her mum was a relaxed, fun-loving single mum who suffered from mental illness. She was diagnosed with depression and medicated with electric shock treatment and up to twenty-seven pills a day. It kind of breaks my heart that all my uncles and aunties and mum have ever said about my grandma is how loving and kind she was, yet she was plagued by mental illness that was given even less support in those days than it is now.

My mum's extended family were intelligent and successful, her aunties were some of the smartest women I ever met. I'm sure I would have thought the same of my grandma if I had had the chance to meet her.

My grandpa (my granny's husband) lived in America, he was in the navy and met my grandma on his travels. It was a strange relationship, since they had a lot of children together but he always lived in the US. I had a bit of a relationship with my grandpa, he would visit us in Australia and once when I was eleven, he flew my mum and me to Seattle to stay with him.

He was a strange man, very straight and uncomfortable with human affection, I remember jumping on his knee as a kid and I felt his whole body tighten up with awkwardness, then as a teenager I kind of teased him by constantly placing my baby brothers in his arms to watch him squirm. As someone with very few physical barriers, I was intrigued by him and his lack of affection.

That kind of life left my grandma's five kids to get away with a lot. Mum was the oldest of three boys and a sister, my uncles were surfie punk teenagers, big-hearted kids who didn't mind getting up to no good and my mum went down the road of early virginity loss and experimenting with drugs.

She first tried heroin when she was sixteen and was addicted by seventeen. Turning eighteen was a huge year for her — she met my dad, fell pregnant, married my dad, and her mum died at the age of forty-two after a battle with lung cancer.

Throughout my childhood, I never really understood how young eighteen really is, I do now.

By the time I was old enough to know anything, I knew that there was a grey cloud that followed my mum's family, there was a lot of heartbreak and I am still amazed by the incredible people who came out of such tough times.

Mum, who had already been judged for her drug use and gossiped about by the extended family, was now in the position of moving into a rental with her husband, her new baby and her three little brothers, in charge of getting food on the table and keeping a roof over their heads. Her youngest sister was only eight and too young for my mum to care for, so she went to live with an aunty, which I know my mum still carries guilt for.

My dad took it in his stride, he had met my mum after moving to Perth to attend art school, fell in love with her instantly and being one of eleven himself, he was happy for my uncles to move in with them. In between sharing joints, sneaking out with them and kind of just being another kid for my mum to look after, he also did his bit to raise and love them. My dad had nothing but pride for this unusual set-up called our family.

My uncle once said to me that "it's a sad story but it's our story".

I never forgot that.

Three years later, I was born, my mum finally kicked the heroin habit and went back to work while my dad worked on and off as an artist.

I obviously don't remember these times but I have visions of my dad sitting in the lounge room on the floor painting with a spliff hanging out of his mouth, my mum breastfeeding on the couch, my long blond-haired uncles coming and going as they pleased and despite the sadness and struggles, I feel it would have been a pretty cool place that I would have liked being in.

My mum worked hard, she showed us that you pick yourself up every single time. Her strength is her power and also her flaw, proud as fuck. Whenever I'm having a proud moment, my bestie refers to it as "Jackie's pride" rearing its head. She hates sympathy, once she was at a cafe and was introduced to a snobby old rich lady who knew my mum's grandfather. She gave her a sympathetic look and said "Jackie? Oh poor Jackie." My mum just got up and left. No time for that shit.

She co-slept with me, told me how amazing I was, never cared that I failed every subject in school and just lived her life alongside me. She had no mum friends, we didn't miss a Sunday session at the pub where we would dance all night — her with her wine, me with my lemonade. She worked on the door for various bands around Perth which consequently meant that I knew most of the guys playing live music wherever we went. By the age of five, I wasn't shy of getting on the stage and shaking my arse while singing the choruses to my mum's boyfriend's tunes.

Throughout my life, my mum has only ever encouraged empathy and kindness to the under-privileged. I never once got away with calling people bogans, or judging someone's family or another kid. She was always a constant reminder of how tough most women have it, that it was important to see the world through other people's eyes — single mums, low-income earners, ex-addicts, alcoholics. My mum, with her slightly communist views, had their backs in life and she opened my eyes every day to a way of thinking that in a privileged white first-world city like Perth felt like the opposite from the norm.

It wasn't until I was older that I realised my mum had passed on a curse as well and I had inherited from her this huge chip on my shoulder towards the privileged. Mum is so anti-rich and I realised that I had spent a good portion of my life hating on rich people too.

Conservatives needed not bother opening their mouths around me, their opinion was of no value to me. Ironically, I didn't realise that I was an even bigger judgmental bitch than the people I was judging for being judgmental bitches.

Then one day it occurred to me, if the advantaged disregarded the disadvantaged the way that I disregarded them, I'd be furious. So slowly I am learning to get over my chip and convincing myself that those who have it all also still have interesting ideas and valid views.

My mum guided me through knowing what being disadvantaged really meant, she drummed into me how lucky I was and how many opportunities I was given that so many others missed out on. She made sure that I will always use my voice to speak for the voiceless, no matter what it was that made them feel voiceless. But the underprivileged or the unwell is as far as her compassion goes.

So now I have been left to push through and extend my ability to feel compassion for the privileged as well — to the skinny, to the beautiful, to the healthy and private school educated. To teach myself that we all have our hurdles, we all have shit going on and what you see on the surface isn't always a great reflection of what's going on deep below.

I still believe that privilege is a responsibility and upon meeting the filthy rich, there will always be that burning question of why do they need so much when we have starving children in the world but that's their path, not mine to judge.

My mum owes me for the therapy that I've had to sit through only to come to the realisation that she will never change, she will never be easy to get along with, her and Bill will probably never get along — she's too protective of her children to get on with their partners. I have complained too much about her to Bill and Bill to her and I guess now I just have to live with it.

But my mum really is the backbone of who I am and when the twins are spewing on me while I'm in the bath and my house is covered in diarrhoea … she's there. She might be in a little huff because she's just yelled abuse at a passing car and her boyfriend's blocked her phone number yet again but she's there. As Bill once said, she'd argue with her own shadow if you left her alone with it. Would I change her? No, well yes. But I can't, nobody can, so we just roll with her punches and focus on her loveable side.

BODY IMAGE — BEFORE AND AFTER BAMBINOS

I was an average-sized kid, my sister was kind of skinny, my mum worked and succeeded at being slim. She believed in the importance of maintaining a slender physique, something I have never judged her for. Being a young, unqualified, attractive single mum of two, she wanted to hold on to her appearance as if a prize possession and possibly a means to pull her out of our financial struggles. Women who capitalise on their looks to better their situation, in my opinion, shouldn't be judged any more than those who invest an inheritance with the intention to better their future. Both didn't work for it, both are making it work for them. My mother is unusually attractive, which is sometimes a blessing, sometimes a curse.

Of course, that rubbed off on me (the skinny pressure, not the ridiculously good-looking vibe — while I do alright for myself, people aren't exactly stopping me on the street to photograph my face). So being an average kid was all well and good, we were too poor for me to sit around eating all day and to be honest I enjoyed my outside time. While, like most kids, I didn't want to be average, looking back, I was.

It wasn't until my high school years that things started to go south (or should I say east and west).

Enter my love affair with carbs and chocolate. I was never a fat teenager, but you don't need to be a fat teenager to be called fat by teenagers and having an incredibly skinny mum who watched what she ate wasn't helping my self-esteem.

The thing about getting fat is that it's completely addictive. Eating truckloads of cake and pasta brings temporary comfort but it also makes you gain weight. The more weight you gain, the more uncomfortable you feel, the more you need to turn to cake and pasta for that temporary comfort.

By the time we get to our age we know this but I didn't have a clue about it when I was a teenager.

To make matters worse, I came from a family of hot chicks. They wore hot chick clothes, my sister in her 90s midriff crop tops and my mum in her fitted dresses. I found myself under a peculiar illusion that my only issue was that the clothes I owned were obviously not mature enough for my womanhood.

You see I've always had this condition, it's kind of like the opposite of anorexia. Anorexics are incredibly thin and look in the mirror and see fat, or believe that they aren't thin enough (I don't know exactly what goes on in anorexics' minds, this is just what I have learnt through reality TV and health education).

But me, I was chubby, bordering on overweight, and I saw a skinny chick in the mirror. Still to this day, I don't see my own chubbiness. I am notorious for entering a clothing shop, grabbing a size eight while some puzzled shop assistant offers me a size twelve. I flick my hair as I walk past her, ignoring the ludicrous offer, only to have to eat my own shit from the changeroom when I call out to her and try to explain that it fits — just "not around the boobs". The shop assistant struggles to hold back her laughter as she hands me the size twelve.

As a teenager, slowly but surely against my mother's approval, I changed my wardrobe. So yes, I was that girl at the school parties, the chubby one with the frizzy hair and over-plucked eyebrows who insisted on wearing a crop top teamed with hot pants. Needless to say, I was shocked by the reactions of my peers. Teenagers can be such shits. Some of them tried to be nice and warn me that my outfit didn't suit" me, others were outright bitches, the boys were the meanest.

I had gone from being a fairly popular kid in primary school, even having snagged my first boyfriend and French kiss, to being the laughing stock of the whole school.

I think that may be where my endless amount of compassion for teenagers comes from, being a teenager sucked for me, it was a lonely and shit experience full of judgments and self-doubt.

I remember the night that I made a pact with myself to get an eating disorder. I was so jealous of anyone in my school who was suspected of having anorexia. Having no grasp on the severity of the disease, I wanted to be the damsel girl who was so tiny and cute that the whole school worried about her, instead of being the fat one in tight clothes.

Unfortunately, some of the most vulnerable kids carry a layer of weight as a form of protection. But of course it does the opposite and exposes them to cruelty that they just don't have the strength for. I don't know what I was protecting myself from, maybe salads and phys ed, but I do look at other teenagers who struggle with their weight with a strong sense of compassion and connection to their woes.

So on this night of my eating disorder pact, I went to a really close friend's pool party. Yeah, pool party, you can only imagine. Everyone was there, I was wearing my usual attire — a tight mini dress. Everyone was jumping in the pool, I went to get changed into my bikini (I know! I was my own worst enemy) and as I walked down the stairs to get in the pool, pretty much thinking I was killing it and trying to pick which one of the boys looked the most like Leonardo DiCaprio (I thought I resembled Claire Danes so we could make out in the pool all night and recreate my favourite scene from Romeo and Juliet), all of a sudden, the boys started calling out. "Nooooooooooo, if Con gets in the pool, all of the water will disappear. Don't do it, Con!! Quick guys, save yourselves!!!" They bombied in the water and made out that they were fish who would die if they didn't have water due to a big fat whale entering the pool and emptying it. Not quite the pool pash scene I was expecting.

Now I can joke about this as much as I want, my psychologist Jasmine did warn me once to watch how I turn painful stories into funny ones as a way of detracting from the emotion and above all to make sure that nobody ever feels sorry for me. While I am an empathy addict, I dry-retch at the thought of sympathy.

That was actually a really mean thing for these teenage boys to say. Tears welled up, I turned around, walked back up the stairs and reached for the comfort of my little black mini dress. I went into the bathroom and distinctly remember staring at myself in the mirror, I was so fucking furious with myself. I was disgusted with my lack of willpower, I couldn't believe that I wasn't anorexic, all I wanted was to be so skinny that people would worry about me. Then and there a fantasy was born, a fantasy that when people spoke about my condition they would all know that it began on this night, at my friend's pool party when those little shit fuckheads who were supposed to be making out with me in the pool ruined my life instead. Out of fury, embarrassment and self disgust, I promised myself that I would become anorexic.

Like the majority of the promises that I make to myself, this one went unfulfilled. I love food way too much and comfort eating had and still has its claws fairly well anchored into my psyche. Still yearning for an eating

213

disorder to become that desirable damsel in distress, which would hopefully not only obtain me a boyfriend but also show those knuckleheads from the swimming pool how hurtful their words were, I developed bulimia.

Bulimia is a strange eating disorder, I don't think I lost a single kilo from it, maybe if the health educator at school had have told the class that instead of assuming that any of us gave a fuck about "rotting teeth", they might have deterred me from it. Instead the class was warned that bulimia can cause as unhealthy amount of weight loss. Bingo. Suited me to a T — I got to comfort eat and lose weight, win win right?

I would usually spew about once a day, nibble on food throughout the day and then eat some ludicrous amount of carbonara and then bring that bitch up. While eating the meal that I planned to bring back up (kind of sounds religious, like I resurrected my carbonara "and the third meal rose again"), I would make sure I drank a lot of water, to keep the food fluid. I often found that if I didn't, it would be too heavy and not come back up. Some food felt like a stubborn brick in the bottom of your tummy, I would be gagging and drooling for a good half hour before accepting that this shit was staying in. Depressed, I'd begin my cleaning mission in the bathroom, it doesn't matter how many times you wash your hands, face or neck, while bulimic I always smelt like vom vom.

So my last few years of teenagehood were spent still mildly chubby and now I also stank of spew. I never got my dream of people whispering about my weight loss, nor did I ever get an apology out of those knob-jockeys from the pool party. Bulimia was about as successful for my street cred as my crop tops and mini dresses. Never again.

Most people I speak to who have had similar experiences agree that bulimia becomes more of a habit than a weight management plan. I wasn't warned as a teenager that it gets addictive, that was probably the hardest part of kicking it for me. Learning to be full and not feel guilty about that fullness.

I did finally kick the habit, realising how little it served my cause, around the age of eighteen. Yet for the next year I would still dabble and occasionally I'd feel the urge wash over me if I was uncomfortably full.

Looking back, I can only be grateful that, while I may always be a slight overeater, I was never really taken over by an eating disorder. With age comes wisdom and with true wisdom comes compassion. I have seen the severity of anorexia and I wouldn't wish it on my worst enemy, it is obviously so much more serious than wanting to wear a string bikini and attract a boyfriend.

A lot of young women, who have at one point in their lives struggled with their weight, develop a weight-loss fantasy. They imagine that all their problems will disappear if only they could lose another five kilograms — I'd get a hot boyfriend, I'd get a cool job, I could make everyone who ever rejected me fucking sorry ... if I could just lose another five kilograms.

That was me and it took me a long time to realise that Hot as Fuck ain't a number on the scales, it's an attitude. Big things need to change in your life before you can embrace your inner Hot as Fuck. Some women need to move away from their hometown, some need to have children, some need to mend their childhood wounds.

After my first baby was born, I was determined to get my body back. I was twenty-five, none of my friends had kids yet, and I had gained twenty-five kilos during my pregnancy.

Any more and I would have been sent on one of those healthy eating courses run by the hospital. A friend of mine gained thirty and was sent to the course, she told me it was so degrading — a bunch of pregnant chicks who may have enjoyed one too many desserts sitting in what felt like a naughty girls' room for cake thieves being lectured about the different foods and the amount you are allowed to eat.

"Now ladies." The skinny nurse would begin by holding up a picture of a piece of pizza. "Would we consider this an ALWAYS food, or a SOMETIMES food?" Cake thieves would look at the ground and guiltily reply "sometimes food".

Although I think my presence at that course could have added a touch of humour, I didn't get the referral.

Bill and I lived in a tiny unit. I had a baby that I didn't know how to look after and I was huge — twenty-five kilos bigger than I used to be. As you can imagine, I felt like weight loss was the only sink-or-swim decision I had left. I chose to swim.

So I began long missions of walking while pushing the pram, I would spend a couple of hours a day walking. I quit all carbs, looking back I actually ate fuck-all and breastfed all day. I shrunk to fifty kilograms and I think my baby gained half of it. Within six weeks, through pressure and fear, I had my old body back.

I still had a wobbly tummy but I was skinny …

For me skinny feels like landing that really hot boyfriend, the hipster cool arty one you have always wanted, the one who dates chicks who look like Eva Mendes and somehow you have convinced him that you're worthy of his commitment, knowing full well that you're not. So instead of enjoying something you have always wanted, you spend every day waiting to be exposed as a fraud and sent back to where you belong — in the gutter with all the other self-doubting losers.

That was skinny me, I knew I had skinny for a good time, not a long time. Anything that requires as much hard work as skinny does for me isn't a natural fit. When you're not in a natural fit (ie hot hipster spunk and me), you are struggling daily, and when you struggle daily to maintain something, you will likely fall off the tightrope.

I quickly got married so we could look back at the photos with pride at me as a skinny bride. Just as I felt like I was about to completely blow out, I got pregnant again so hardly anybody noticed, except other Queens of course, who would see me shoving down half a cake at a cafe, pat their own bellies and wink. Sisterhood.

My second pregnancy was similar to my first, this time I was fifty-six kilograms when I fell pregnant and I gained another twenty-five. It became apparent how unrecognisable I was when someone asked Bill "where Constance is" while giving him a judgmental look for having dinner with this random fat chick at our local Chinese restaurant. Halfway through a huge mouthful of fried rice, I had to put my hand up and interrupt, "it's me, Constance," as a grain of rice tumbled out of my mouth and landed on my belly.

After I gave birth to Arlo, like a drugged-up junkie, I once again put pressure on myself to lose the baby weight. This time, however, I managed to do it slower with more consistency. Things were slowly but surely changing for me, I had two children now, a lovely reminder that I was put on this planet for a greater purpose than being skinny.

My weight settled around sixty-one kilograms, a very healthy weight for my height.

It was with the twins that things really changed. When I fell pregnant, I was about ten kilograms heavier than skinny me yet I felt fine with it. Rumi and Snow were both huge babies, even though they were out six weeks early, my body was what some people might consider "ruined". But when you have had two huge babies, two placentas, two umbilical cords and millions of litres of fluid in your uterus, you become pretty much grateful to simply be able to breathe once they are out.

I was now a mother of four, Bill and I were in a terrible place, sometimes we were together, sometimes we were apart. Throughout my whole pregnancy, I was looking forward to my usual weight-loss routine, to give me strength, independence and hope for the future.

But things just seemed different this time. Exercising was harder, the preparation to get Billie-Violet to school, the twins good to go out in the double pram, with a skateboard attachment so that Arlo could stand on it and complain for the whole "power walk", I was exhausted before I even started my walk. Then looking into the pram and seeing one of my little squish heads looking back at me with a cheeky grin, you can understand why I would often change my mind and simply lie on the grass, consuming myself with baby love instead.

The weight gradually came off. I love eating healthy foods, I just don't love being a fascist about it. Remember the addictive cycle getting fat was? Eating truckloads of cake and pasta for temporary comfort, which makes you fat so you feel more uncomfortable and then desperately need the comfort that pasta brings?

Here is my holy grail of insight: Have you ever put on loads of weight and had someone comment (in my world that someone is usually your mother), purely out of "concern", that they are worried about your weight gain, or buy you some new fad diet book or register you for some twelve-step program to help you lose the weight. How does that make you feel?

Does it make you jump on the treadmill and go burn up those calories? Does it make you put the cake down and get your shit together? I mean it's not like you didn't know that you had gained weight, most of us are the first ones to notice. While your friends or family may have convinced themselves that they mean well, most of the time their concern has the opposite effect on your weight, making you feel even more miserable and more uncomfortable, more in need of that comfort food. So off you go to refill your bowl with pasta for the third time that evening.

The only real way to break the vicious cycle of weight gain is to gain comfort in your body without needing it to change. What if you eat for comfort, it makes you gain weight and instead of feeling more uncomfortable, you appreciate your body, appreciate your skin, love the fuck out of that fat roll, which is a representation of the meal you absolutely enjoyed and needed at the time.

So if you notice a Queen has gained some weight, tell her what a goddamn rock star glorious sex beast she looks like and see if by offering some comfort, making her feel better about herself, it will do more good than telling her something she already knows.

I need to keep my weight in a healthy realm, since if I am too big, I lose energy and get too tired to look after these four kids. Even though I think I may be sexually attracted to carbohydrates, staying away from grains does make me happier and gives me more energy. While I passionately hate exercising, life with four kids is fairly active anyway. My drive for skinny, my weight-loss obsession, my belief that all my problems would disappear if I could only lose five kilograms, that has gone.

Thank god for children to remind us of what really matters in this world. I can guarantee that if any of us was diagnosed with a terminal illness and given a month to live, there is no way we would think "hmm, I wish I was skinnier during my time on this earth". We would want to spend our time wrapped up in the passion that we feel for our loved ones.

We and only we can rob society of its expectations of us.

WHAT IS BEAUTIFUL?

When you hear the word "beautiful", what comes to mind? I personally think of a view — an ocean or a landscape. I am in love with the diversity of our planet. I want to travel, see different terrains, I want to see wild oceans, ginormous deserts and I want to swim in a tropical lagoon beside a rainforest.

What happened to the diversity of women? Why are ripples in an ocean mesmerising yet ripples on a lady's tummy a turn-off? Why are the lines on the trees in the woods hauntingly beautiful, yet those on a woman's face should be covered? Why is the Grand Canyon celebrated for being grand, yet Queens are expected to be as small as possible?

Queens' bodies have moved away from a diverse and unique representation of nature and become a product. Eyes should be big but noses small, bums big but stomachs small, boobs big but ears small, lips big but ankles small. Where the fuck did these rules come from?

We are expected to change our skin tone, our hair colour, our lip colour, the colour of our eyes … because beauty? Would you dare to look at a sunset and wish that it was green instead? Would you have the nerve to look at a rainforest and imagine it more beautiful if only it was pink? Of course not, why would we fuck with nature, nature is beauty.

Well, you are nature.

The physical expectations put on women to encourage "beauty" are doing the exact opposite. They are encouraging women to all look a particular way, yet we are so lucky that we don't because we are all tiny diverse representations of the wild, grand, rippled, dark, smooth, round, shapely, wrinkled, bright planet that we come from.

What a beautiful gift, that we are all planted with a seed of our magnificent world, we all represent a uniquely different reflection of this universe and our job is to let that shine.

So why the fuck is society telling us that we should all look the same, that we should cover it or change it or at the very least be ashamed of it. Who the fuck is society to rob us of our individual reflection of this almighty land we were born on?

Queens, we can't do it anymore. So here are our viable options:

1. We can all go and live on a commune together, where we eat berries and our boobs are free to flap around against our hips and we walk past each other high-fiving with "looking rad, babe" affirmations.

2. We can change the society we live in.

Because I am so fucking tired of Queens thinking that they are too fat for that bikini or too old to wear that mini dress, or too ugly to go out without make-up, or our hair's too thin or our legs are too short, boobs too saggy, teeth too yellow, or whatever the fuck society has lead us to believe. I'm sick of it.

We have every right to look in the mirror and feel beautiful, because we are. Each of us was planted with the exact same amount of beauty, except society has only let a particular demographic shine.

My plan is to choose option two — to change society, we can do it together, for all of us, for our children, for our future. We will all shine and reflect the beauty that was planted inside us.

Knowing this and believing it are two separate issues, knowing can be immediate while believing may take time. I always revert back to that saying of "fake it until you make it".

Pretend to love your body until you do. Look in the mirror every day, think about the universe, think about beauty, think about nature, think about chubby teenage me in my mini dress strutting around at a party. Say something to yourself, something kind, something loving. Tell those belly rolls that they are goddamn sexy little bitches, tell your tummy that you wouldn't have it any other way.

Think about the things that have "ruined" your body. When my brother was four, he told my mum that her tummy looked like a testicle, it was hilarious because it did, it was saggy and wrinkly, but that testicle tummy gave her four of her main reasons to live. Your breasts may sag around your ankles, how amazing is that? They breast fed and were the main source of nutrition for your little cubs. Your smile lines represent a life of laughter. Extra seven kilos? Hello?? This fucking legend enjoyed every single mouthful of those seven kilos.

The majority of the things that we hate about our bodies comes from places of love and joy, isn't it ironic that women are conditioned to regret and feel guilt over the things in their lives that have brought us joy?

Fake it until you make it, Queenie Bees. I live by this mantra, I apply it to a happy marriage, success in parenthood, career, everything.

Because I am not an expert on anything at all, everything I appear to be successful in has actually been faked so well that I get to a point where I look back and go, "hang on, I actually did this, it wasn't fake at all".

This works with body love, you can learn to hate your body quite easily, all you have to do is flick through Instagram, a magazine or watch TV. Society is making body hate a fairly instant and easy practice.

Body hate comes naturally in our society, while body love requires a conscious decision. Make that decision now, life is way too short to spend it wishing that you looked a certain way, the universe is way too powerful and magnificent for you to hate its creation.

Faking it until you make it is the first step:

1. **Tell yourself that you love the way your body looks**, every day remind yourself that you are now an expert on body love.

2. **Pick a different part of your body to shower with compliments** every single day, treat that body part as if it was a vulnerable little cherub who doesn't understand its own worth. "Morning, tits. Do you have any idea how glorious you are today? Thanks for softly hanging around me and making my torso a better place."

3. **Never say anything negative about yourself to anybody.** Treat your body like it is your best friend, would you bitch about her every opportunity that you had? Speak about your body the way it deserves to be spoken about, like a highly intelligent, desirable temple of love.

Your brain follows your mouth, do this for six months and your brain will believe the things you say.

All of this positivity can only rub off on your family, too. Remember that we are leading our kids by example, they do as we do, not as we say, they pick up on body guilt and body shame.

Bill drools over me, my post-baby pouch and box slap (which is kind of like a box gap only instead of having a gap between my thighs, I have a slap sound as my thighs embrace each other when I walk), my flat bum and my over-sized nipples. He tries to grab a feel every single time I pass him, because when a woman is swanning by nude, knowing that she looks rad as fuck, all you see is brightness, all you see is pride, all you see is love.

Don't we all deserve that Body Love.

SURVIVING SCHOOL

If I had known that graduating primary school would be the biggest academic achievement of my entire life, I would have paid more attention.

I was twelve and not a particularly talented or smart or sporty kid, just a kid with an imagination and an unrequited taste for romance.

You don't receive merit awards for having the most number of crushes on boys, so while I believed myself to be a major undiscovered talent, I certainly wasn't on the receiving end of too much teacher attention.

My primary school graduation had three awards: 1) the dux, self explanatory, the smartest little fucker in the school. 2) the runner-up dux, second smartest little fucker in the school and 3) The honorary end-of-school "award" for general legendaryness.

I can't really explain the astonishment on the entire school's face when I received the Legend award.

Like there was no clapping, just silence and tumbleweeds of confusion. I hadn't even had a merit award since year three and that was only a sympathy "shit we forgot about Constance" award. The principal only remembered me as the girl who spewed in the hallway after eating an entire tub of zinc cream yet when he tried to call someone to pick me up, nobody answered. The deputy principal knew me as the girl who had been called into his office after being complained about by three parents fed up of me prank-calling their sons at all hours of the night — bitches had no appreciation for passion. I think I winked at him on the way out of his office too … cringe.

So as the awkward silence turned into a round of applause, I bowed, finally feeling appreciated, went back to my seat and basked in my own glory.

My mum, who after months of begging, took a half day off work and made her very first (I'm exaggerating) appearance on the very last day of the very last year at the school. She couldn't help but ask my teachers what the fuck that award for her under-achieving daughter was all about and my teacher replied with the following: "Constance received the award out of kindness. She didn't think I noticed but one day the girls were drawing in groups. Con sat with her usual girls and Stacey (a girl with special needs) took her usual spot on the floor by herself. Constance got up and invited her into her group, Stacey said 'no thanks' and Con insisted, finally Stacey went to

225

sit with Con and they giggled and drew together even though the other girls now moved away from Con too. I watched from my desk with tears in my eyes and decided that this award was going to her."

My mum was so proud, she valued sweetness over maths any day, I was confused but certainly not complaining.

I can still remember the day the teacher was talking about. I wasn't a particularly kind kid, like most kids I thought about numero uno 99 per cent of the time, but something just didn't sit with me, I couldn't bear to see Stacey colouring on her own. The funny thing was that I thought that teacher actually hated me. Years later working in a pub I served her husband a pint of beer and he told me that I was his wife's favourite student of all time. My skin tingled with goosebumps, I had never thought I was anyone's favourite anything until that day.

YOU CAN WRITE

When I was seven, I wrote a poem for a school project. Looking back, I have absolutely no idea where the words sprouted from, I couldn't possibly remember it word for word but it had a cold feeling and was based around nature. There was definitely a line in there somewhere that said "The wind and the trees are my only friends". I think I was attempting to sound deep or troubled to give my fellow second graders a taste of my mystique.

I was so goddam proud of my poem, I read it to my teacher, she tried not to laugh, I read it to my friends' parents, I read it to everyone at lunch time. I bumped into my teacher from the previous year in the hallway on my way to the toilet, low and behold it was on a piece of paper in my pocket and I asked her if she wanted to hear it, she nodded with glowing eyes. When I was finished, the beautiful kind teacher looked me straight in the eyes and said these three words: "You can write."

My early adult years were spent with a notebook constantly in my hands, there were no smartphones, and it was part journal, part calendar, part art. Sometimes I look back at my journals and see how I subconsciously used them to prevent anxiety. If I felt myself getting panicked in public, I would focus on writing something and slowly distract myself from the rush of anxiousness which would usually turn around and creep away when I managed to stop focusing on it. Nowadays I possibly do the same with my iPhone.

Words have always come to me in forms that gave me a need to string them together on paper, the way most women put together outfits. I'd like to take a step back and evaluate whether or not they worked.

The first "blog" I ever did was written from an apartment where I was renting a room, next to Park Guell in Barcelona. It was kind of cute in an almost derelict way, the neighbours had naked children running wild through the hallways and strung their washing out on their small balconies. I would run a mile from the Australian equivalent because "bogan" but I felt romantic in this Spanish squalor, because "cultured".

I was nursing one of many broken hearts when I arrived in Spain, I had just been dumped at Brighton train station by one of the only people I knew in London and made the split-second, irrational decision to buy a one-way ticket to a place I had never been to and knew nobody in — Spain.

Nothing ignites creativity quite like a combination of heartbreak, loneliness and Spanish wine. I had been armed with a diary since the day I left Australia and now in this apartment, alone, I noticed that my new housemates had left their computers unattended.

So I transferred some of the romantic dribble about the foreign streets, my lonely heart, the people I had begged to employ me illegally, my unquenchable thirst for adventure and wine from my moleskine diary to an email, an email that I sent to every contact in my email account, from flight centre workers to high school friends to random spam accounts … Send all.

Cruising the streets of Barcelona in a pair of thongs, a big skirt, singlet and head scarf (symbolic of my gypsy theme, as without it I was just a bum), I walked into a mini supermarket by the beach and was faced with a confusing decision.

I had one euro and that was it. Well, that's a lie. I had one-hundred pounds in my shoe at the place that I was renting, that lucky sum had been travelling with me for sometime and despite not having a return ticket home to Australia and having no money to pay my next week's rent, with no visa to allow me to work, I was under the strange impression that that one-hundred pounds was my safety net so had refused to spend it. So from that point of view, in the mini mart on that day, I had one euro.

Decision time, I was starving and thirsty. I hadn't eaten since the day before when one of the South American guys that I was renting a room off had brought home leftover sushi from the sushi bar where he worked. Once he fell asleep, I scoffed half of the feast before rearranging it to cover the holes.

I had a choice, my one euro could buy me one of two things: option A) a banana and it looked like a good banana or option B) a dodgy-looking pink plastic razor. My armpits were becoming a problem, I have never liked sleeves, the second the sun peeks out from behind a cloud I have been driven to expose as much of my skin to it as possible. So now in this incredible sunny land after being in London for a couple of months, I was desperate to enjoy the sun — except my armpit hair was beginning to dreadlock.

I stood there for a moment, ear phones in listening to a random Spanish radio station that every now and then would reward me with the familiarity of an American song. Weighing up my options, my tummy grumbled with such intense hunger yet I didn't feel like I had a choice. I didn't know anyone in Spain, there was nobody to call and ask for help.

So I made the most strategic decision I could think of … I bought the razor. You see, without a work permit, without a dime, without knowing the language, I couldn't see any way of earning myself any more money to pull myself up and out of this hole. The one resource I had at my disposal was my looks. I was thin at the time and consistent with the repetitive theme in my life, my skinniness offered me a false sense of security.

I believed that I could use my looks to secure myself a man and the man would buy me as many delicious bananas as I wanted. You can give a woman a fish and feed her for a day, teach a woman to fish … or however the fuck that saying goes. But I wasn't going fishing with hairy armpits, so I bought the razor, shaved my pits in the public toilets and continued my day, walking down to the beach.

Sitting on the beach, looking at the water, connected me with the family that I missed. It was a softly crashing reminder that far away in Perth, Australia, they swim in this very same water. I remember feeling very far away from home as I tried to ignore the voice of my anxiety telling me how well and truly fucked I was.

Then, all of the sudden like some kind of Latino mirage, I was approached by Roberto. A long-haired, dark-skinned, head-band-wearing dreamboat.

I could have pinched myself, I was obviously being well and truly rewarded for not buying the banana.

Roberto asked me if he and his friends and cousins could join me. He could barely speak a word of English, so we communicated through a Lonely Planet Spanish to English booklet, which in a few weeks I would learn was a blessing as he and I were definitely not destined to be soulmates. On the odd occasion I was able to translate what he was trying to say, I would be irritated beyond belief, but hey … I needed fish, Roberto would become my rod.

It's a fine line between being a young lady in need, capitalising on opportunities that present themselves to you and being a prostitute. A few times in London I went out to dinner with English men I wasn't attracted to because I was hungry, once I slept with a really overweight Puerto Rican guy either because I needed somewhere to sleep or his accent was cute, I certainly didn't judge myself on that decision the following night when I slept at the Liverpool train station.

Turns out Roberto lived in Madrid with his female cousin, he was extremely attracted to me (thank you bald armpits) and both of them were desperate to learn to speak English. Bingo, I am your girl. They knew I had no money and offered to give me free accommodation in Madrid and food in return for my English wisdom.

I survived the rest of the two weeks that I had paid rent for on barely nothing, I befriended a guy who owned a pub and he let me hand out flyers for pub crawls to tourists on La Rambla for five euros an hour. It got me through, although I did have to break my trusted one-hundred pounds into euros to buy my bus ticket to Madrid.

Roberto and his cousin lived in a nice clean apartment not far from the train line and the city. Their parents who lived in Venezuela paid for it while they studied in Madrid. He and I started sleeping together, physically I was really attracted to him, mentally not so much … We had no future, partly due to the fact that Roberto had no past. While I am happy for anyone whose life has been blessed with no hardship, on an intimate level it's virtually impossible to find a place to connect with them. As a girl who went out of her way to torture herself on a quest for soul, I was left feeling kind of flat after every poorly translated conversation that I had with Roberto — his favourite movie was The Mask for fuck sakes.

He left me at home all day while he would go to a private college and study some sort of filming course. I would go out, walk the streets, sit under a tree and write for hours, go to the parks, but would inevitably tire of it. I became tired of being alone, tired of waiting to see if Roberto would take me out, tired of not having my own money and living off someone else. No matter how many "English" lessons I was giving him, his annoying nature drove me crazy and I finally decided I hadn't been given a fishing rod at all, I had been given a fish, every day a fish, and I wanted my fishing rod. It was time to go home.

The decision to return home was a tough one for me, had I been away long enough for everyone at home to believe that I was "worldly"? Did I prove myself capable and exotic? Would I be believably cultured upon my return? So many confusing questions.

How I would get home would again prove difficult, since I had no return ticket, no money and no job. I wouldn't ask Roberto, even I was too proud to give the little silver spooner that satisfaction.

So I arrived at the Australian consulate, assuming I would simply wave my passport around before everyone dropped everything they were doing, sounded an alarm that called the limo and red carpet to whisk me on a first-class flight back home because, as the media had led me to believe, displaced Aussies are of great importance to our government. Sitting in Roberto's apartment while he repeatedly watched different scenes of The Mask, almost falling off his chair in hysterics, had left me feeling remarkably displaced.

You can imagine the rude awakening I received when the consulate was full of displaced Aussies, in fact the consulate was turning them all away with nothing but a free phone call and glass of water. I saw Aussies there in states worse than you see on early Sunday mornings on Oxford Street, some looked like they had been waiting there for years.

I accepted my free water and began the journey back to Roberto's apartment. I knew I only had one option. My dad was broke, my mum was broke, my brothers were babies, I had nobody to ask but my faithful sister Stella, the only family member with a full-time job, she even had this thing called "savings" because her shit was so well and truly compacted together that she was buying a house. An upbringing of "have-nots" gave Stella a fierce determination to become a "have" and she was well on her way. The only thing holding her back was that annoying little sister, the one who continuously fucked up her own life and required bailing out.

I had been dreading the day I had to ask her to fly me home, she knew it was coming, she had sent me texts whenever I had a phone number to give her asking me if I was OK, she had even called me crying once saying that she couldn't stand not knowing where in the world I was. When I was an apprentice hairdresser earning $180 a week, Stella paid my annual $500 school fees, she'd let me live in her apartment rent free. Stella was definitely going to bring me home and I would pay her back, I always did, I respected and appreciated every little thing about my big sister.

When I returned to the apartment, I turned on Roberto's computer and logged into my emails for the first time since I had sent out my group "blog" to every single contact in my account. I was not expecting to see so many responses. Everyone was so overwhelmingly entertained by my account, some found it hilarious while others found it profound. Me? Profound. Fuck.

One friend whose opinion meant the world to me sent me an email and I was filled with pride when I read the three words: "You can write."

My sister begrudgingly agreed to bring me home and bought my ticket, leaving the following day. Roberto was sad, he survived, I suspect through some more Jim Carrey masterpieces. I arrived back in Australia where I no longer had to choose between armpit hair and food, my fishing rod was at home, my independence, my travels had given me a great appreciation for my right to work. Uncultured as I may have been, I was certainly changed.

Writing about my life had become my life.

BEING JUDGED

When I was a little girl, my dad would pay for me to come and spend my Christmas holidays with him. My sister and I would fly over all by ourselves and have the best time with my dad and his family.

People used to always ask me if I saw my dad and when I told them that I spend my holidays with him, they would reply telling me that he must be such a good dad. They were right — he was. He would save up his money because he loved us so much and didn't want years to go past without seeing our faces.

But at that young age I was often curious as to why nobody ever told me that my mother was such a good mum?

She did what my dad did, she worked hard, she changed my bed sheets, she made my school lunches, she helped with my homework, she cooked and cleaned, she made sure that I never went to school without a braid in my hair and that I had a clean school uniform. She did that all year while my dad did his part for three weeks of the year. Not only did she never get recognised, but she was condemned for having different boyfriends, for working full time, for having a social life on the weekends. My dad worked, he had different girlfriends and a social life all year. But he was a good dad and my mum was a questionable mum.

A friend of mine, Bronnie, broke up with her boyfriend Dave before their baby turned one. She got a mortgage, moved into her own house, went back to work and basically just went on as you would expect any hardworking hero mum to go on.

When their daughter turned five, Dave would pick her up on Fridays after school and take her back to his house for the evening.

Everything was fine until the mums at school started telling Bronnie that she was so lucky because Dave was such a good dad. "I see Dave picking up little Lucy every Friday and I just think, god he's so involved, such a great dad."

Now Bronnie was a little baffled, why is he such a good dad? Because he picks up Lucy from school once a week? Why is the "good dad" badge so goddamn easy to earn? While she slogs her guts out to create a world for Lucy, take her on an overseas holiday, finish a degree while working full time so she can get a promotion, nobody's calling her a good mum.

A couple of weeks ago I bumped into my friend, Clair, in the shopping centre. She's a divorced mother of two boys. Her ex, Steve, moved to Melbourne five years ago, while she lives in Perth with four-year-old Kai and nine-year-old Archie, who has autism. Whenever I have spent time with Clair and her boys, I have bowed down in total worship for how patient and resilient she is with Archie. He can be quite violent, anxious and easily fall into a zone that only his parents can get him out of.

So when I asked Clair how she was, she responded that she'd had enough. "I can't mother Archie at the moment. When I think of the fact that I am going to have to mother him for the rest of my life, I fall into a deep depression."

"Oh no! So what are you going to do?" I asked.

"Steve is going to take him in Melbourne for a few months, he has agreed to doing it. I'm already stressed at the idea of not having him but I just can't go on. Archie has become dangerous for Kai and even me to be around, he has completely worn me down."

"Well, I completely understand, I don't know how you've managed for this long, you're amazing. You need a break, he'll live with you again. Don't think of it as goodbye, you'll see him all the time."

"I wish everyone was as supportive as you, my mum isn't talking to me, the other mums at school have stopped inviting me to Friday arvo park drinks, Steve thinks I'm the shittiest mum ever. I mean fuck! If I had have done what he did and bailed five years ago, I would have no friends and no family. I can't believe the judgments I'm getting."

When I left Bill, I went out a lot. I felt like I had been married and mothering for my whole twenties and I was craving some freedom.

Unfortunately, I hadn't quite figured out that freedom doesn't lie at the bottom of your second bottle of wine.

The only social life in our marriage had been Bill's and I was certainly making up for it now. Boozing on, seeing different men, I still cringe when I think about some of the states I found myself in.

I had most of the custody, that wasn't even a question, with Bill taking them every second weekend and one weeknight a week. Bill was happy for this but the third day every second week was inconvenient for his work and he would often say that he couldn't do it.

I had worked out that my hairdressing business was losing on average $1000 a week from me having to fit in with the kids' kindy and daycare hours. If the kids were sick from school, it was my responsibility. Buying school uniforms, doctors' appointments, swimming lessons, homework — all my job.

I didn't mind, I am a bit of a control freak when it comes to the kids, I was just grateful that he would take the children when he said he would. So on my days off, I'd party. Tragic partying to distract myself from the state of my life but partying none the less. And fuck was I judged.

I even had a friend say to me: "Don't you think you should calm down and relax, poor Bill is at home with the kids and you're always out. Shouldn't you be putting the kids first?"

Every second weekend? To clarify I had the children ALL week (minus one night) and every second weekend.

How quick my friends were to forget that I had been at home for

years with my kids, breastfeeding, night waking, no job, while Bill
went out with his friends, while his career flourished, while he partied.

But "poor Bill" is stuck at home with the children every second weekend
when really it should be me, all the time. And don't you worry about Bill
… He was having his share of fun, my Billy Boy is not one to sit down
and feel sorry for himself, in between nursing his broken heart, he pretty
much relived his entire glory days.

Women judge each other so harshly. We hold each other up to the highest
most self-sacrificing standards and expect absolutely nothing from men.
Have men been such letdowns for so long that we throw a little party
every time one cooks a fucking meal? Have women been such martyrs for
so long that our expectations of them are this ridiculously high? I hear the
term "supermum" being thrown around as if it's something achievable, I
am yet to hear the term "superdad".

Are women so overwhelmed by the expectations we are putting on
ourselves that when we see another woman taking steps to make her life
more enjoyable or easier or more fucking fair, we need to tell her that she's
not doing the right thing because otherwise our own unhappiness won't
feel justified.

But the sad thing is that it's not, our hard work and misery are not
justified. We should be standing together and saying no more. I won't be
the second priority in my own house anymore. I won't put my career on
hold, even if I don't make as much money as my husband. If I want to
work, if I want more of a social life, if I want more child-free time to see
my friends or take up a course, I will.

I used to think to myself that if I was single, I would have more free time.

Bill would have to take the children sometimes and give me a break. Why was I fantasising about leaving my husband to have a life again, couldn't I have a life and husband?

Maybe then we wouldn't feel so jealous of divorced women out there killing it at life, because we would be too. There is no shame in putting yourself first. Dads do it, we can do it too.

Women are easy targets for other women because there are so many self-sacrificing Queens out there to compare them to. I say, let's stop comparing, Queens are doing their best, we are all dealt completely different hands, some of us aren't even dealt anything at all.

Let's just drop it, judging another Queen isn't doing us any favours, it is simply justifying our own unhappiness by telling ourselves that she is a shit mum when she's not, she's a Queen.

Ask yourself some serious questions: Does her happiness trigger resentment? Are you happy? And if not, make some serious changes. Because you deserve to be happy.

Don't ever forget that a divorce is when Queens need each other the most. Some of us go off the rails, some of us get really snappy, some of us make everyone else jealous by constantly winning at life. But all of us need support.

CHAPTER 9
Uniting the Sisterhood

Before I had kids, I wasn't exactly a girl's girl. I mean, I had my friends and I loved them but I spent a hell of a lot of time drinking beer with blokes. I think this had more to do with the fact that I loved drinking so much and most of my girlfriends were way more responsible than me. For some reason they didn't see the joy in spending twelve hours at a pub on a Sunday, fucking weirdos. So while my "besties" were still Queens, my network was guys. It feels weird saying that now that I'm the world's biggest Queens' Queen.

Do you remember that try-hard girl in high school who would do anything to get in with the cool group? The one who hated smoking pot because it gave her anxiety yet would punch a bucket bong with more professionalism than Cheech and Chong just to be in the cool group? The one who you would feel sorry for but not quite enough to risk association with and reach out an empathetic hand? Well, bitches that was me. I was the try-hard girl prepared to do anything to be accepted. Somedays that was achieved by being the class clown and others it was by giving a guy a wrist job behind the school shed. They were tough years.

Rule number one for a high school girl was fit in or fuck off. There is a pack and if you didn't join it, you'd be left behind.

Queenhood has a different approach, you don't have to be anything like each other to be a Queen. By the time a lady reaches Queenie status, she has done it all and she has absolutely no fucks to hand over to anyone who expects different of her. Self-acceptance is Queen.

Queens are too individual to stereotype, you get those really loud, over-sharing types who, like myself, aren't afraid to ask for help, cry to strangers and tell anyone who dares to insult them to fuck off. And then there's your understated, introverted, shy Queenie Bees who like to keep their cards close to their chest and take a while to warm up to the pack. Some Queenies are immaculately dressed and others like myself can't seem to find matching thongs and regularly do school runs in their PJs.

The fact that you are a Queen is all that you need to fit in. It doesn't matter how far distanced you have been from the sisterhood of Queens, once you are ready to join, there is a branch near you ready to accept you.

I wish I knew this when I had my first daughter, she came into my life and for the first time I felt purpose. But with that job came an overwhelming loneliness — a loneliness that Bill couldn't fill.

I hadn't been the best friend to my Queens, they didn't have kids, I felt like they didn't understand me, I felt like nobody did. I never went to mothers' group, I was so scared of not fitting in. I was so scared of the conservatives, the judges, the perfect parents. I often felt like I blinked and everyone around me was rich with immaculate interior design and perfect marriages. I didn't even have a cot, I had to put a post on Facebook to see if anyone had one they weren't using.

I had no idea that the whole point of Queenhood is that you don't have to fit in, you just have to be there.

I had no idea at all how absolutely imperative it is to be in a Queen pack, I had no idea how much love and support and laughter would come with one, I had no idea how desperately I needed my Queens, for healing, for intimacy, for connection.

Having a baby will make you thank your lucky fucking stars that you have a vagina, or what's left of it anyway. Because only other vagina owners can be there for each other in the ways that we need.

Men try, they really do, but unfortunately they don't know exactly how it feels, which leaves them only being able to offer us sympathy. How do you feel when you get handed a dose of sympathy? Like shit. Sympathy feels like someone is looking down into the shitty space that you're in and calling out "Hey there, that's a really shitty space, you poor thing" and you're there covered in your own shit looking up at them in their bright shiny space going "OK thanks for that, glad you stopped by, now please fuck off".

Queens offer empathy, when someone knows it because they have felt it, they aren't looking down at you in your shitty space at all, they climb into it with you and say "Wow, this is a shitty space, it looks like mine.

I've brought two bottles of wine, let's get some glasses and we can laugh about how shitty our spaces are." And you know what, that might actually be the only way out of your shitty space, realising that you're not alone. I can feel the weight lifting and the sun shining through from knowing that I am not alone.

If I could go back to that time, the time when I had my first baby, I would spend less time feeling like I didn't deserve to fit in or to be a parent or like some kind of a fraud for having the title of "mother". And I would spend more time doing this one thing, this one responsibility that comes with our crowns (I know I hate the word responsibility too, but this is fun) — I would reach out to my Queens.

Call them, walk over to them in the park, introduce yourself, have a sleepover at your aunty's house, make your girlfriend come and sleep over at your house. Every single day you need to ask yourself, "How did I reach out to my Queens today?"

Your relationship with your Queens is such an imperative one, it will keep you sane, sisters must stick together. All of that self-doubt that you feel, all of that uncertainty, we are all feeling it, we are all feeling like big fat failures with anxiety and relationship disappointment, we are all sitting here at school drop-off worried that everyone has noticed that we aren't wearing deodorant. We need each other so desperately.

Some people envision power to be aggressive, a storm, the indestructible physique of a well-trained man, an armed force. This power is designed to instill fear into its enemies, with a flex of the muscles and a reminder of who's boss.

However, without fear, all of those images of power crumble.

And fear isn't real …

Power is not forced. Power is not brutal. Power is not fear.

Power is soft, gentle, sweet and kind.

An empowered woman is not just the woman who kicks arse in her corporate job, it's not just the woman who owns her house mortgage free and doesn't need to rely on anyone for anything.

An empowered woman is a kind woman, one who sees the beauty in another woman, one who lends her hand to a fellow woman, one who empathises, one who recognises her own unique beauty.

Power is subtle.

Nadia, a mother from Billie-Violet's school, asked me if I was OK one day. I was wary, she is attractive and drives a nice car, I was low and that made me suspiciously assume everyone had bad intentions.

Never one to hide my feelings, I blurted out that I wasn't OK, my life was actually a bag of dicks at the moment. She responded by introducing Arlo to her daughter, Heidi, and asking him if he wanted to spend the day with her at their place. When I looked puzzled, she replied: "You need me. Arlo and Heidi are going to be best friends whether they like it or not, you need a break, go out on your own, sleep all day. Enjoy yourself."

That kind gesture carried so much power, power that gained so much momentum that today our bond is strong, indestructible.

Vulnerability is empowerment because it is real. Nobody can pull the rug out from underneath vulnerability because there isn't one to pull. That is powerful, that is true independence. Vulnerability is power disguised as weakness.

We are tested when we come across vulnerability, how we respond will determine our empowerment.

Once I asked everyone I knew to take the kids for me for a couple of hours, my mum was at work, Bill was at work, I had to get to a last-minute specialist appointment. Nobody said yes, my pride stung, it was the first time I had ever asked, people had always said they were there to help, but when I needed them … Nobody.

I won't forget the feeling of reaching out and being rejected. Nothing makes you crawl back into your shell like reaching out and being met with a "no".

I vowed to do whatever I had to do to stop women from coming to me for help and being met with a "no".

Now I am that woman, the one who has a trail of her own four kids and then three other people's kids following her, and I love it. Other people's kids are hilarious, they keep my kids entertained, nine times out of ten they are better behaved than my kids.

That is power, in all of its kind glory. I feel like an army. Because I am the lucky one, I can get to know all these divine little souls and I know that there are vulnerable Queens out there that I am helping, like I've been helped. A powerful army of love and sweet kindness. That's the shit that conquers the world.

Empowerment at its finest.

BUILD EACH OTHER UP

Why are we constantly tearing each other down?

When I started blogging, I promised myself that I would never tear another woman down, there is enough of that in society. Everywhere we turn, a woman is being held down until she believes that is where she belongs.

I'm not saying that there aren't Queens out there doing things that I don't agree with. If one Queen is doing something that will make a whole bunch of other Queens feel like shit about themselves then yes, I don't agree with it but I have promised myself that this will be a black-and-white rule — no tearing Queens down.

Instead I will spend my time building up the other Queens, the ones who have been trodden on, played against one other, the ones whose self-doubts have been exploited to benefit society.

Ignore the shit and reward the good.

So I found it really hard to get my head around the fact that Queens are still tearing each other down around me. It happens all the time at school pick-ups, everyone is bitching about each other, or even worse everyone is bitching about one particular Queen.

You hear it from those P & C mums who are clearly a million times better than the rest of us "can't be fucked" mums, and all those keyboard warriors on Facebook who seem to crack a slippery clit every time they see a post that has a tiny hole that they can poke their "I'm a better mum than YOU" sign through.

Why, especially on my page that I have built entirely on Queen praise, on Queen saluting, on tipping the crown to each other as we create a mass group of Rad-Bitchness, why are Queens still tearing each other down?

So like with all of my big questions, I tossed and turned on this one for a whole night, I really didn't want to accept that it might come down to the fact that a lot of Queens are just mean, who love bitching and making other Queens feel like shit. I love women too much to believe that. So praise the lord when I woke up graced with the answer.

Women have been oppressed for thousands of years, we are still repressed today in many ways. The facts speak for themselves, men are still getting all the good jobs, men are still making all the good money, rates of domestic violence are still soaring out of control, feminism is still needed in so many ways.

The modern-day women has had to fight for everything she wants. She is fighting society's pressures and the lack of value attached to her role.

So when you are being held back and you desperately want to break free, to be up there, in the light, where you belong, how do you suppose most women are getting there? They are climbing on top of one another to get out, they are using other women as a stepping stone to give themselves a boost and help themselves break free of the patterns that we are born into. They don't even know that they are doing it.

What makes things worse is that we are being told that we have equality. How many times do you hear a keyboard warrior or some chauvinistic pig telling us to not complain, because "women in the Middle East are being stoned to death" or "in Vatican City women still can't vote", or "in Yemen women aren't allowed to leave the house without their husband's permission". So stop your whinging women, you can vote and get an abortion, that's enough for you. First world problems.

I find it ironic that people are still having to compare us to some of the most barbaric practices in the world in order for us to feel "equal".

Women are feeling overwhelmed. Recent studies show that a mother who works full time is still coming home to an average of six hours of child-care and housework duties every day, that full-time working women are getting paid about 18 per cent less than men and doing twice as much of the home duties.

If you are angry, you are allowed to be, although that doesn't sound like much fun to me either. You are allowed to complain, you should complain, if you don't want your daughters to find themselves in the exact same position that you are in. This has nothing to do with the stoning of women in the Middle East, this has nothing to do with women's rights in Yemen. These examples are thrown at us only to silence us because all of those people (men) who are getting the extra income, who are getting the cool jobs with the cool cars and coming home to half the housework you do, they don't want to hand over their cool new car, they don't want to come home to a pile of dishes in the sink, they are going to do whatever it takes to silence you.

But Queenie Bees won't be silenced.

So when Queens are being held back by all of these external pressures that society has convinced you that you don't actually face, it's only natural for a woman to see her fellow women as a way to make herself feel better, to use another woman as your stepping stone. I don't believe we would do it to each other if we were given an even playing field.

So for example, you see Queen Jess at playgroup (now we know I'm making this up because I never once went) and she's just loving herself sick, life's good, she's had a blow-dry, her clothes fit, she's talking about her trip to Broome and instead of being happy for her, you can't help but compare yourself to her thinking, "great, I have baby spew in my hair, I can't afford to pay my bills, I just want to go home and roll a big fat spliff instead of sitting here and listening to that smug bitch talk about her bullshit holiday".

Now an hour later when Queen Tania comes along and tells you that Queen Jess' life ain't all that, she may be rocking that blow-dry but word is that when she was in Broome, her fella was getting a blowjob from her sister, she's taking a bottle of Valium a day and wishes she was dead.

We feel so relieved that Queen Jess' life actually sucks as much dick as her sister does. So off we go to gleefully validate our own shit existence by gossiping about another Queen's downfalls, using them as stepping stones to make ourselves feel better.

But guess what, Queenies? Our unhappiness doesn't need validating at all — we are entitled to it. People expect way too much of us, our lives have been filled with the most unrewarding jobs, thankless tasks, we are working too hard for not enough money, we are being played against each other via advertising campaigns. Even the fact that our bodies are so superior that they can create life and then go on to feed that life has somehow been used against us.

We should be angry.

So now when I see a keyboard warrior, tearing down another mum because she bottle-fed or she dared to go out on the weekend without her children, instead of getting furious that she is daring to judge another Queen and make her feel terrible, I think to myself: "That poor Queen, society has torn her down, expected too much of her, made her feel like she isn't enough for too long. Now she feels like her only way out is by using another Queen as her stepping stone to help her climb out of here."

But that's not the only way out. If you are using other Queens' hardships to make yourself feel better, we will never change society. The only way we will find ourselves living in an equal society is by doing the exact opposite, the opposite to what every channel, every ad, every website is telling us to do.

Drop the competition, forge a oneness between women, break down the barriers, stick it to society by saying: "No. I will not tear down other women anymore, no matter who they are or what they are doing. I will not be a part of this vicious cycle of mum shaming, bitching, stepping on a fellow woman to make myself feel valued or worthy. Because I am valued and I am worthy. I do not need to validate myself with other women's hardships."

United we conquer, divided we fall. Queen Power. Bam. KEEP YOUR EYES OPEN FOR A QUEEN IN NEED.

It's easy for us to always want to be in the cool group, the sexy bitches with their cool clothes, that group of school mums who seem to have it all, the funky mums, the professional mums, the funny mums, the confident mums. Remember that popular group of high school girls that you always wanted to be a part of, well, they seem to have reformed at school drop-off or playgroup and now you're dying to be accepted again.

The exclusive groups, however, aren't looking after the Queens in Need, in fact in my experience they are the ones stepping on Queens, in need of that constant reminder that they are doing OK. I met a group of mums once, I was that loser high school student showing off trying to make them like me and it worked, they did.

There was also this really sweet shy Queenie who sat on her own all the time waiting for her kids, always offering a smile. I chatted to her a few times, she was sweetness through and through. One day I casually mentioned to a member of my cool crew that I really liked that shy mum.

The Cool Queen nearly lost her tampon, she laughed so hard. "Her?" she replied. "I know her from my school days, she's really feral and always stinks of BO, she needs some deodorant."

As the rest of the coven cackled, I couldn't help but think back to my high school friends, the ones who would only like me if I punched cones and handed out blowjobs to football players. I wondered where they ended up, how far being a cool cunt got them.

Luckily, I know that they were only using the shy Queen to give themselves a boost and make their own armpits seem fresh and I don't know if I actually trust anyone with fresh armpits ...

Anyway, that Queen, the one who doesn't wear deodorant, is still my friend today, she is sweet and kind and loyal and we need each other. I'm not saying that the cool Queens are cunts, saying shitty things doesn't make Queens cunts, it just means that they are having shitty days and we all have them. What I'm saying is don't forget about the Queen in Need, the one on her own, the one with the weird haircut, the one who has BO or drives a bomb. Because in my experience you could be the one missing out if you don't reach out to her.

The Sisterhood is all inclusive, it is about raising our vibration as Queens and sticking together. They will try to divide us to conquer us, they will try to convince us that we are not repressed but they won't win. My drive to seek out my Queens is far stronger than anyone's repressive beliefs and expectations of me. I won't buy into the dog's bollocks that I am being fed, the shit that's designed to divide the sisterhood, because it is, we are, stronger than that.

Look at everyone's situation with compassion, as when all else fails, compassion still wins. Don't forget that the bitchy Queens who are stepping on you or other Queens, tearing us all down, they need the sisterhood the most. Reach out, every single day, reach out for them, reach out for you.

We were not put on this planet to feel alone, togetherness will set us free. That togetherness will bring love, the only thing that can cure the pain from the past is love in our future. We've got this Queens.

DEPRESSION AND ANXIETY

"Constance Hall glamorises depression."

Somehow that was supposed to be criticism!!! I found that little beauty as a comment on a news article after my blog got some attention over a post I shared on anxiety. I loved it!! Because while I have never been diagnosed with depression, my anxiety has been fairly debilitating at times and I have felt depressed a lot. So you can only imagine how my inner Queen beamed at that statement.

Just because we are depressed and freaked out and struggling to leave the house without Valium and Ventolin and a bag to spew in, does not mean we aren't glamorous, so why not glamorise depression!! Crowns, ladies.

A lot of people are shocked when I tell them that I suffer from anxiety, as I don't look like I'm suffering from anything, I come across incredibly confident and capable … most of the time anyway.

That's what makes anxiety such a clever little bitch, it convinces us that it needs to be hidden from the world, convinces us that it is not a condition that happens to us, convinces us that we have acquired it through weakness and inadequacy, thus stopping us from letting anyone know it's there.

I like to think of anxiety as an abusive partner or ex, when you're out being fabulous, winning over a crowd with your incredible charm and enviable humour, it rears its ugly little head and whispers in your ear: "You're a loser, everyone's looking at you, thinking you're a big fat loser." But you have to pretend he's not there so that you don't expose yourself as inadequate or weak, so none of your friends can do what warrior Queens would do when they sense their girl is being hassled by an ex-partner and race to your rescue by kicking its arse.

Well, I'm here to tell you that if you are suffering from anxiety, you don't need to keep it a secret at all.

Suffering from anxiety is nothing to be ashamed about, only really clever, hilarious, deep-thinking, well-dressed legends with cool hair get anxiety. FACT.

Be proud if you are one of us!! But together let's fuck the "suffering" off.

When I went on Big Brother at the age of twenty-one and made a national disgrace of myself for ten days, getting booted out for lying about my relationship status and being a general fuckwit on television, I started to get kind of anxious. Weird, I know.

There were a lot of contributing factors to my anxiety at the time, contrary to what people may think it wasn't brought on by embarrassment. It took years for me to realise that I didn't actually kill it on the show, I honestly thought that I was a fucking rock star legend and the country simply wasn't ready for my awesomeness. Now looking back, I realise that at times I was just a little dickhead, but who isn't at that age really.

Self-forgiveness is the key.

I think being a twenty-one-year-old binge drinker who didn't have a job probably contributed more to my anxiety. The fact that one out of every ten people I walked past on the street called me a wanker could have had a tiny bit to do with it but I usually laugh at haters, so I'm going to blame the borderline alcoholism and unemployment first.

As my anxiety became really bad, booze would bring me a stability, stop my hands from shaking and ease this strange suffocation feeling, so I would drink a lot more.

I explained this to my doctor one day when I made myself an appointment to whinge about my anxiety. Instead of prescribing me the Xanax I was asking for, he was pretty spot on when he pointed out that while drinking alcohol can temporarily ease anxiety, it makes it worse the following day, which is where you get into that cycle of drinking to cure the anxiety that you have from last night's hangover only to feel worse the next day and so on.

Before you know it, you're in rehab teasing a big beehive into your hair to try to make the best of a shit situation while singing Back to Black — only you can't sing, you're basically just mumbling to yourself with knotty hair. Not ideal. And certainly no Amy.

Despite this only being a phase — not forever, nothing is forever — the seeds of my anxiety were well and truly planted, only rearing its little bitch head again when I began my two-million-year breeding stint. Over the next few years, I would gradually collect small pieces of my own shit until eventually I had all my shit together. Killing it.

Once I fell pregnant, I stopped binge drinking (shock horror I know) and a lot of my anxiety had already calmed down. It was nice, I had so many other things to doubt myself over by then that I really didn't need it.

Postnatal anxiety isn't talked about as much as postnatal depression but it should be. So many women I know, even ones who have never suffered anxiety before, start to get symptoms after pushing out a baby. It's surely no surprise, after cruising the world kid-free with nobody to worry about except your legendary self, your biggest fuck-ups consist of — but are not limited to — forgetting that you have a tampon inserted when about to shag a freshy you met at the pub or lighting the wrong end of a cigarette while trying to be sexy (drunk/ sexy is still sexy).

Now all of the sudden if you stuff up, someone — and not just anyone but your most important little king, queen or snuggly-alien — could die. If that doesn't make you nervous, I'm not gonna call you a "relaxed natural", I'm gonna call you a total freak. You are the one who needs psychiatric evaluation, not me and my debilitating anxiety. I'm a rad bitch.

So now that we have ascertained how absolutely normal anxiety is, I want to share with you one of the most helpful pieces of advice that I have ever received, something that I think contributed mostly to mine having gone right where it belongs … away.

This advice originally came from my aunty Lisa. Aunties are so important, full of love and wisdom, we should all spend more time with our aunties.

Firstly, let's not call it an anxiety attack, that's such an aggressive term. I have made it very clear that only rad bitches suffer from them so from now on we refer to it as a Queen-down.

I was getting a lot of Queen-downs when I first took my baby home. It was scary, I didn't want to do anything one-on-one with people because with that sort of intensity, I knew that I would reveal my true self and they would learn that inside I was not coping or trying not to shit myself, vomit or pass out.

Remember how anxiety is just like an abusive boyfriend, well imagine that said abusive boyfriend knows what your biggest fears are and teases you with the threat that it may happen. Of course I have never just shat myself at coffee, ordered myself a soy chia latte and vomited on the counter and I probably never will, but that won't stop my abusive boyfriend (anxiety) from trying to convince me that it could happen.

Because socialising is fun and leaves you feeling refreshed, it helps you feel strong and kicks anxiety on the arse on its way out the door. So why would your abusive boyfriend want you to do that? It will go to any lengths to stop you.

If you have ignored the fucker all day, it will throw in the big guns with a Queen-down. So how do you disempower it?

You, my Queenie, are the boss and like any good boss lady would, it's time to disempower your enemy. First step is as follows: Anxiety wants you to keep it a secret, so do the opposite. Tell everyone who will listen: "Hi, my name's Constance, I have four kids and still look this fabulous. I get really bad anxiety so if I pass out and vomit on your shoe, just keep on as if nothing's happening, I'll be fine."

You won't get strange looks because everyone will totally relate and tell you about their own struggles or be too fucking jealous of your Rad Bitchness. The most important thing to remember is that people in general are very kind and possibly most of the ones you pass on the street have had or are having their own battles and have had the Queen-down before, so they are around to help.

There are Queens everywhere, some you know, some you don't, just waiting for a Queen in need to help.

If you find yourself in the midst of a full-blown fucking Queenie-Bee down, the whole world needs to back the fuck up now, just be a total fucking diva about it. Ask yourself, what would Constance do? "I can't fucking breathe!! HELP ME. Take my baby, get me water, I need to lie down, put a cushion under my goddamn head, EVERYBODY PLEASE STOP TALKING AND HELP ME!!!"

I am telling you Ninja Queens will appear, with their walkie-talkies (OK iPhones but walkie-talkies sound more secret agent). They want to help you, tell you to lie down, be a diva, get the help that you need and deserve. Your anxiety will hate it, it will hate me for telling you to do it because you will realise that you have nothing to be afraid of and if anxiety loses fear, it will find itself with very little power.

Secondly, you need to ask yourself, what's the worst that can happen? I'm always scared that I'm going to shit myself. I have dodgy bowels so it's highly likely that when I feel nervous, I will need to do a poo. My anxiety knows this, like all abusive exes there isn't much about me that it doesn't know, so when I'm walking into an intense situation, it whispers in my ear: "Don't forget you could poo yourself at any time … Imagine what your new friend will think of you if you poo yourself."

Now that is a scary thought, right? Pooing yourself at a hipster cafe while a bearded, tattooed coffee maker with black rim glasses screws up his nose and the equally-as-cool waitress with her funky haircut slips in your steaming pile of turd. I'd do whatever my anxiety told me to do just to avoid that scene.

But the reality is quite different, I have been there. It was gastro week, the kids had finally gone back to school, twins in daycare. I was so proud of myself for being the only family member to remain gastro-free. While everyone else suffered on the couch, I skipped around admiring my health and preaching to the family all things probiotics and green smoothies (I think I have drank one green smoothie, chased with a Coke, so I don't know why I was on this high horse). But my gastro was there, just lurking in the shadows waiting to attack at the most inconvenient hour.

So in the hipster cafe, with my mum, halfway though my soy chai and my tummy started grumbling. I looked for the toilet but there was no time. I braced myself and swiftly moved towards the Queens' toilet. Debating whether the swift long stride movements that weaken your bum muscles and force your business out quicker were worth getting to the toilet faster. Discussion over, it was coming out. I could no longer run... I had to stride. Striding through a cafe with a shit coming out of your bum is interesting. Watching everyone to see if they know ...

I finally got to the toilet and guess what? It wasn't a big deal. I popped my undies in the bin, cleaned myself up and nobody was the wiser. Of course Bill got off on laughing at my story when I got home, Miss Probiotics Green Smoothie shat herself at a hipster cafe. But that's all it was, a funny story.

So there anxiety, I am no longer scared of your threats that I'll poo myself and a hipster chick will slip on it and my new friends will judge me.

That's not the way pooing yourself in public goes down.
Suck shit, Anxiety 0 Queenie 1. Boom.

This can be applied to every different type of Queen-down, what is it that
you're anxious about? Anxiety tells you that you might pass out and make a
fool of yourself? Who cares, in reality passing out would be glorious, think
about the help from strangers. Don't get me started on the sexy man you
could land on. How relaxing, like a little nap in a cafe or supermarket.

So show it that you believe it is powerless, you have evaluated all of its
threats and come to the conclusion that it has no power over you anymore.

Don't let anxiety convince you that the fact that you're suffering from it
makes you an outcast, you would be seriously surprised if you knew how
many of your friends are suffering too. Tell people, disempower your anxiety
by doing the one thing that it doesn't want you to do. Tell everyone it's here
and it's trying to mess with you. Queens are your army, they will conquer
your anxiety if you let them.

Despite talking a lot of the time about how depressing my life is, I have
never been diagnosed with postnatal depression.

Every single time I have brought a baby home, I have waited a couple of
months for things to start looking up, they haven't and I have taken myself off
to the doctor's for a PND evaluation. Every single time the doctor seems sure
that I'm OK and can get through it without meds. Yes, I did end up begging
for Valium and basically got dragged out of his office — still no drugs.

While I was pregnant with the twins, I prepared myself for PND — I was
sure I'd get it this time. I went to the doctor's, asking for anti-depressants
because I wasn't coping. I was crying every day, throwing things at Bill, I felt

ashamed of my lack of parenting skills with the other kids and I couldn't see any light ahead.

Thankfully through a twist of fate, I saw a relief doctor, not my usual one who tends to treat me like a drama queen. This doctor referred me on to my psychologist Jasmine. She saved me.

Only on the day of my appointment, I was so nervous that I nearly cancelled. However, one thing that I have learnt from years of anxiety is that if something makes you nervous or anxious, it is imperative that you do it. So I walked into my very first-ever solo counselling session. Jasmine's office is at the back of her house in an affluent area. I assumed she would dismiss me as a tattooed pregnant punk who deserved every second of her misery.

Was I wrong! Jasmine was the Queen I needed. She may have looked conservative on the outside with her lovely blow-dried blonde bob, but deep down she was a tattooed-up rock star. To break our barriers, she told me about the time she shaved her head and did her rock'n'roll rebellious years. That helped me, as every time I sat in her beautiful limestone office with immaculate furniture, I would imagine that Jasmine was a rocked-out punk with piercings and inked sleeves and we were just two punks having a casual chat waiting for our Es to kick in. I felt so at home.

As soon as her warm face looked at me, I burst into tears.

"I married a massive cunt."

"My kids must hate me because I'm such a lazy cow."

"They're gonna grow up to be serial killers because I don't hug them enough."

"My family is off the fucking hook, I can't even begin to tell you how mental my mother is."

"Bill's going to leave me and I'll never, ever, ever meet anyone else because I'm a fat psycho."

Jasmine responded: "And breathe."

I breathed.

Our therapy continued after I had the twins, having babies can be really depressing. I think it's worth it, I have never been happier than I have since having my children but there are some really dark times and lonely times when you're learning how to deal with your new life. So many contributing factors — lack of sleep, lack of socialising, incredible pressure, anxiety over your baby's health. I'm going to be completely honest, it's a miracle we come out of it alive.

In my darkest times, this piece of Jasmine's advice was so extremely helpful, that I want to share it with my Queens.

Face-to-face socialising is the best therapy you will ever do.

Even when you don't want to, even though it is so much easier to stay home and watch Oprah with a packet of chips and stalk ex-boyfriends on your iPhone, you must go out and socialise. Call a friend, even if you don't know them very well — force yourself to do it. As often as you can, even though getting a baby in its car seat, packing bottles, nappies, wipes and a spare change of clothes can totally suck. (Tip: I don't bother doing any of that, I only said it to sound efficient — I merely put the baby in the car seat and hope for the best.)

You will feel lighter, more capable, the small insignificant shit that you have been worried about could wash away. Your friend could be going through the exact same shit and you might both sit there cackling like witches at how depressingly hilarious your lives are.

Jasmine will be very proud to know that you are out there, breathing.

So if that abusive boyfriend (your anxiety) tries to convince you that you can't make it, you just can't socialise face to face today, that you're too anxious or nervous, remember to disempower it and go. Nothing is as important as getting out of the house, confiding in a friend, laughing. Fuck the dishes, fuck the washing, just go.

And please Queenie, don't forget, anything that makes you nervous or anxious is undoubtedly worthy of your time.

MY PARTING MESSAGE
The world needs Queens, we have a battle on our hands that requires our optimum health.

Quit smoking.

Get your bloods done regularly. A general blood test every six months, so you know what's going on in there.

Get your boobs checked, even if you think you are "too young", you are not. Get them checked.

Have your pap smears as soon as they are due. Without fail.

Look at your poo. I have an inflammatory bowel disease, which makes me the Queen of checking poo. Bill does not appreciate me standing outside the toilet asking for every detail of his poo but poo is so important. A healthy poo is whole and complete with no blood, it sinks to the bottom of the toilet and is a medium brown colour. Other types of poo may need diet alterations and sometimes doctors.

Eat good food (quit dairy).

Wear condoms. Like shoulder pads, HIV is not just for the 80s.

Keep your relationship with stress dignified, since fearing stress only stresses you out more. Accept it, say hi, pour it a glass of wine and ask it to leave before it outstays its welcome.

Hassle your husband. Women nag for one reason, we know best. Men don't go to the doctor's enough, nag them. Because even though they snore and hide in the toilet for forty-five minutes and follow us around the house with a stiffy most days, we don't want them to die.

Find a doctor who you want to see, one that you have a good relationship with. After reviewing my abortion history, I once had a doctor refer to my new baby as a "lucky" baby, as in having escaped death by termination. I was shocked. Needless to say, I was not giving her the honour of diagnosing my infected in-grown arse hair, thank you very much. So I found a funny one, he laughs at my jokes, he doesn't judge and he cares about my health.

Recognise the excuses you make to stop yourself from going to the doctor's. "It's probably just a cough" or "it's probably just an internal haemorrhoid" or "these constant headaches are probably just from stress". Stop making excuses and get them checked out. The sooner you find shit, the sooner shit gets better and we can go back to saving the world.

The world needs change.

Corruption and suffering and greed have ruled for too long.

How are we feeding our children three different dinners, trying to get one spoonful down their fussy little gobs while another child lies in the dirt, taking his last breath while starving to death?

How has loneliness taken over an over-populated world? How have we become so disconnected from one another that we can no longer hear each other's cries or feel each other's pain?

Queenhood is a movement of connection. A Queen's eyes and hearts are open, we won't ignore the suffering anymore, we won't comply when we are told to keep walking, or when we are told to change the channels.

I am asked time and time again, what makes Queens Queens, what does a women need to do to become a Queen?

Firstly, there is no initiation process. Queens aren't waiting at the other end of a pile of coals with a crown in our hands. I do not choose who is a Queen, neither do you.

We are all Queens. The gift that I will always be grateful to have received is that I am able to see crowns. I see Queens (like the kid from The Sixth Sense who whispers "I see dead people". That's me, peering out from a doona whispering "I see Queens, sometimes they don't even know that they are Queens".) I see them through crown-coloured glasses and will never take them off.

That crown offered you the gift of Queenhood and through Queenhood you are able to:

Help where you can help and where you can't help, support.

Queens are the most powerful demographic in the world. Our hearts have been specifically crafted, knocked around, bruised and broken. And all that did was gift us with compassion. It is no coincidence that Queens have the biggest hearts, it is no coincidence that you find yourself crying at a Kleenex ad or not being able to shake that vision of starvation in the Third World. Just like it is no coincidence that you are reading these words right now. The universe has lead you down your specific path and your unique experiences make you the Queen of your very own kingdom.

Maybe you have been a drug addict or a prostitute, have been sexually discriminated against or were abused by your parents, or maybe you have had your heart broken by a football player who gave you the clap, or lost all of your money to an online scam. Your experiences, your hardships — no matter what they have been — have turned you into the Queen of that domain and nobody in the world is more perfect for the job of ruling that path than you and your compassionate heart.

You were put through that for a reason and you are reading this for that same reason. Because empowered women are the saviour that our world needs.

They say that the world needs a hero, well they are wrong, the world has millions of heroes — they simply need reminding of their power.

Queens will save the world.

Every time you are expressing kindness, handing over some of your wage to a charity, giving another Queen a compliment, recognising a lonely Queen and taking the time to get to know her, offering to babysit for that single mum at school who's doing it all on her own, sacrificing your coffee money for that homeless guy who waits at the train station every morning, choose to understand instead of judge.

You are changing the world. Every time that you are connecting yourself to someone else, you are changing the world.

Queens are the change the world needs.

This, Queens,

Is just the beginning.

You did all the hard work yourself, you got yourself here and after all the blows, all the tears, all the sleepless nights, all the unappreciated hard work, all the years of self-doubt, you have earned that crown. It is your entitlement, your birth right, this is who you are. A Queen.

Bitchiness and competitiveness and vanity need constant feeding and you Queen have cut off their life supply so just like that, they disappeared. Your power did that.

Now that you know that your self-worth is this high, that all the things you have been conditioned to give a fuck about have disappeared, you are left with this clarity, this euphoric knowledge that you are here to rule this kingdom.

You didn't read this book by coincidence, we didn't all come together online by coincidence. We are here to change this world and we are starting today.

So Queen, what are you going to do with all this power? Queens know that power is responsibility and as one your job is to bond this sisterhood, help this Queenhood, support the needy and show the ones who don't know who they are yet that they are Queens. You are the messenger.

They are your sisters, some are struggling, some are rocking out and they are all your Queens, beautiful and full of love.

The ones who behave in the most unqueenly ways need their Queens the most, they are just hurting. You are the opposite of hurt, you are love. Flood them with it.

Buy that Queen who's struggling a week's worth of school lunches, introduce yourself to that Queen sitting on her own, take that Queen's baby off her hands for a few hours, start a roster for picking up kids from school to help Queens get back into the workforce. Start picnic dinner nights where you all bring the night before's leftovers to the park for all the kids to share, it saves cooking and unites Queens. BAM.

What is the unique gift that you can bring to this Queenhood?

How do you know what your calling to the Queens is? What inspires you? What is that particular thing that you can't look away from when you see it? You owe it to yourself to learn more, to become who you really are because you need to pass that on. You don't need a degree or a job, you don't even need to take your PJs off, all you need is the one thing that you have, your own power.

Do you love writing? Can you leave beautiful notes of encouragement or can you start an online group for local Queens to connect? Do you love painting? Can you have a kids' painting day at your house to give Queens a few hours to themselves and inspire creativity in our little Kings and Queens? Have you always loved doing hair? Brilliant Queens love having their hair done, get four of them over and deal with their regrowth. Love cooking? Cook for fuck sakes — cook for us all!

Discover what you love so you can share it with the Queenhood. Take photos, write posts, take to social media. I firmly believe that kindness is infectious, so tell the world and hashtag #queensunite and watch this grow.

The most important skill that a Queen has is her ability to see Queens. Queens see beauty, Queens see hilarity, Queens see kindness, Queens see talent, Queens see Queens.

Because what you see in others is what you see in yourself.

You need to show that Queen that her patience with toddlers is admirable, you need to tell that Queen when you notice that she has an incredible knack for interior design, that you think she should take up painting, that her clothes are always so well put together, that she has the best sense of humour, that she always makes you feel good about yourself, that she's glowing, that she's led the most interesting life and she should write about it, that she is a Queen and you are in awe of her.

Let this spread like wildfire.

Queens are a force, people will try to stop us but not once will they succeed because love, kindness and unity is backed by the almighty universal wisdom, they always win.

That is your gift and it keeps giving and giving and giving.

Grab this Queens, run with this Queens, we have each other, we have everything we need.

This is our kingdom and we have chosen to fill it with love and I am so excited about our next chapter. We are doing this together.

You started this by being you.

A Queen.